WINNING LEADERSHIP TEAMS

MINI'IMAH SHAHEED

for those who lead

❖

*to my eldest son, Isa, who taught me that life
itself is a labor of love*

PREFACE

Leadership is both an art and a science—a delicate balance between strategy and intuition, vision and execution. Over the course of my twenty-three-year journey as a professional educator, and more recently as the CEO of Georgia's largest network of public charter schools, I've learned that the foundation of every thriving organization is effective leadership. John Maxwell's words ring true: "*Everything rises and falls on leadership.*"

This truth has shaped my career and inspired me to write this book. Leadership is a journey of constant growth, marked by victories—both big and small—as well as moments of profound learning born from pitfalls and challenges. I've had the privilege of leading diverse teams, guiding others toward their potential, and navigating the intricate dynamics of organizational change. Through these experiences, I have come to a certainty: to accelerate the success of organizations doing good in this world, we must strengthen the leadership teams that drive them.

While this book is written from my current seat as a CEO, its lessons are universal and applicable to leaders at all levels. Whether you are leading a team of two or two hundred, serving as an executive, manager, teacher, or aspiring leader, the principles within these pages are designed to meet you where you are. Effective leadership is not reserved for those at the top—it is a daily practice that transcends titles and hierarchies. Wherever you find yourself on your leadership journey, this book offers insights, tools, and inspiration to help you lead with intention and impact.

In fact, *Winning Leadership Teams* is more than a book; it is a call to action for leaders at every level to reimagine how they lead themselves and others. In its ten concise yet impactful chapters, I invite readers to explore the principles and practices that underpin exceptional leadership. This is not a text burdened with theory alone—it is a practical guide, rooted in personal stories, rich reflections, and actionable strategies. From the power of self-reflection to the nuances of accountability, coaching, and creating a culture of feedback, this book offers leaders the tools to unlock their true potential and transform their organizations.

Throughout the narrative, I draw on a rich tapestry of influences: African proverbs, childhood memories, everyday moments, and hard-won lessons. These elements are woven together to create a leadership philosophy that blends introspection, collaboration, and strategic foresight. My goal is to equip leaders not just with strategies but with the mindset needed to navigate the complexities of modern leadership with authenticity and purpose.

One intentional decision I made in writing this book was to keep it concise—approximately one hundred pages. As a CEO, I have often found myself struggling to finish longer leadership texts. Time and attention are precious commodities for leaders, and I wanted to create a resource that would be accessible and impactful for leaders at every stage of their journey, from the novice to the seasoned expert. This book is my gift to the leadership development space.

As you turn these pages, my hope is that you will find inspiration, clarity, and actionable insights to fuel your own leadership journey. Whether you are building a team, navigating a challenge, or simply seeking to become a better version of yourself, I invite you to embark on this journey with me. Together, we can reimagine what it means to lead teams—intentionally, authentically, and with unwavering commitment to excellence.

Welcome to *Winning Leadership Teams*. Let's get to work.

CONTENTS

1

LOOK IN THE MIRROR
– THE
IMPORTANCE OF
SELF-REFLECTION
IN LEADERSHIP

I n 2018, my life was thrown into a whirlwind of uncertainty when I was diagnosed with an aggressive form of triple-negative breast cancer. The diagnosis was a brutal wake-up call, a jarring moment that brought my entire world to a standstill. It wasn't just the physical toll of the disease that I had to face—it was the emotional and psychological weight of it as well. While I focused on battling the disease with all my strength, seeking treatment and trying to heal physically, I was also drawn into a deeper, more introspective search for meaning. I couldn't help but wonder if there was something more beneath the surface of this diagnosis—something metaphysical, perhaps, that could offer insight into my journey.

This search for meaning led me to Elle, an energy healer whose approach to healing went beyond the physical realm. Through her gentle guidance, I was introduced to the idea that breast cancer—particularly in the left breast—can be associated with an imbalance in self-love. At first, I resisted this notion. After all, how could I, a driven, accomplished, and determined woman, be someone who lacked self-love? I had worked hard to achieve success in my career, to lead others, to build something meaningful. My life was full of tangible achievements, and I didn't see how my success could be connected to a lack of self-love. Elle didn't rush to convince me. Instead, she gently encouraged me to peel back the layers of my life and my identity. What we uncovered together was something I hadn't fully realized before: my relentless pursuit of achievement, my constant striving for perfection, had created an emotional barrier—a subtle but profound neglect of my own emotional well-being.

Elle offered a prescription for healing that initially felt alien to me—almost foolish. She suggested that I stand in front of a mirror, look deeply into my own eyes, and say aloud, "I love you. You are enough." At first, I resisted this exercise. How could something so simple and vulnerable possibly make a difference? But I trusted Elle, so I tried it. The first time I stood before the mirror, I was shocked by how unfamiliar my own reflection felt. I had never really seen myself in that way before. It was as if I was looking at a stranger. In that moment, I realized how little I had ever truly connected with myself—not just physically, but emotionally and mentally. For the first time, I saw how disconnected I had become from the very essence of who I was. That simple practice of looking into my own eyes and speaking words of love was, in its own way, a powerful reckoning. It became a pivotal turning point in my journey— one that would forever change how I understood self-love and leadership.

This experience taught me that true self-love is not about accolades, accomplishments, or external validation. It's about embracing who you are in the quiet moments when no one else is watching. It's about showing up for yourself, without the need to prove anything to anyone. As leaders, we often focus on projecting confidence, competence, and authority to the outside world. But how often do we pause to look inward and understand what's happening within? How often do we take the time to reflect on our inner world, our emotional landscape, and our personal truths? This practice of "looking in the mirror," both literally and figuratively, became a cornerstone of my leadership journey. It offered me invaluable lessons that would shape my decisions, my actions, and my relationships with others.

Leadership is often associated with bold decision-making, strategic visioning, and the ability to inspire and rally teams toward ambitious goals. The image of the CEO—confident, strategic, decisive—is pervasive in our culture. But while these outward qualities are essential for success, they are only part of the equation. Beneath the visible actions of a leader lies a quieter, less celebrated practice: self-reflection. The ability to look inward, to question oneself, and to learn from one's experiences is just as important as making bold decisions. It's a practice that can make or break a leader's ability to grow, evolve, and create lasting impact.

This chapter is about exploring the transformative power of self-reflection—a practice that is both deeply personal and essential for effective leadership. It's a journey I've come to know intimately, shaped by a life-altering health crisis that forced me to confront myself in the most profound way. Through my work with Elle, I discovered that leadership is not just about leading others; it's about leading oneself with honesty, integrity, and compassion. True leadership begins with self-awareness and the willingness to engage in continuous personal growth. This process of introspection fosters authenticity, a quality that is vital for building trust and inspiring others. Leaders who lead with authenticity are more likely to build lasting connections with their teams and to create an environment where everyone can thrive.

Embracing your strengths

Effective leadership begins with understanding and celebrating your strengths. As leaders, it's easy to fall into the trap of focusing solely on our weaknesses—on what we need to improve or fix. We are often conditioned to think that leadership is about overcoming our flaws and becoming the perfect version of ourselves. However, this mindset can be limiting. Recognizing and celebrating our strengths is just as important. When we acknowledge what we do well, we empower ourselves to lean into those strengths and use them to bring greater value to our teams and organizations. For me, one of my greatest strengths has always been my ability to connect with people, to inspire teams, and to navigate complex challenges with grace. These strengths didn't come from a place of ego, but from a deep understanding of what I was naturally good at and how I could use those gifts to serve others.

Self-reflection is key to this process. It allows us to identify and name our strengths—not as a form of arrogance,
but as a tool for intentionality. When we know what we're
good at, we can amplify those strengths and use them strategically. This doesn't mean ignoring areas for improvement,
but rather it enables us to approach our growth with greater
focus and clarity. Leaders who are aware of their strengths
can harness them to create a positive impact, both for themselves and for their organizations.

Identifying areas for improvement

While it's crucial to embrace our strengths, it's equally important to confront our areas for growth. Effective leaders
are always learning, always evolving. Early in my career as
a CEO, I realized that my intense drive to deliver results
sometimes overshadowed my ability to withhold judgment.
I was so focused on achieving success that I didn't always
take the time to be patient with others' flaws or fully appreciate their perspectives. This gap in my leadership was
something that Elle helped me identify. She taught me that
identifying areas for improvement isn't about self-criticism
or beating ourselves up, but about humility and a willingness to grow.

Self-reflection requires honest introspection. It involves
asking tough questions: *What are the gaps in my skill set or
knowledge? What feedback do I consistently receive from others?
What patterns keep showing up in my behavior or decision-making?* Leaders who embrace this practice demonstrate a level
of self-awareness that inspires trust and respect. They are
not afraid to confront their weaknesses, because they understand that growth is a continuous process. Self-awareness
allows leaders to adjust their approach and become better
versions of themselves over time.

Healing professional wounds

Leadership is often shaped by our past experiences—both the triumphs and the setbacks. For me, my professional journey had been marked by a series of challenges and setbacks that I had not fully addressed. These experiences, while formative, had left scars. Sometimes, I carried these wounds into my leadership, allowing them to influence my decisions in subtle ways. There were moments when I hesitated to take risks or second-guessed myself, afraid of repeating past mistakes.

Through self-reflection, I was able to confront these wounds. I took the time to understand their origins and to process the emotions tied to them. This wasn't an easy process—it required vulnerability and courage. But it was necessary. Leaders must confront the parts of their journey that hold them back, whether those are past failures, regrets, or unresolved pain. By doing so, they transform these wounds into sources of strength and resilience. The scars that once held me back became symbols of perseverance and growth, reminding me that leadership isn't defined by perfection, but by the ability to learn from the past and move forward with greater wisdom.

Confronting fears

Behind every leader's confident exterior lies a layer of fear. Fear of failure, fear of inadequacy, fear of rejection, or even fear of success. These fears can shape our decisions and influence how we show up as leaders. During my sessions with Elle, I learned to confront these fears, rather than let them control me. Naming my fears gave me the power to address them head-on.

For me, one of my biggest fears was not living up to the expectations of those who believed in my leadership. I feared disappointing my team, my family, and even myself. By acknowledging this fear, I was able to address it directly, rather than letting it unconsciously influence my actions. Confronting fears is not about eliminating them—it's about learning to move forward through them. This practice builds resilience and helps leaders develop the courage to make bold decisions, even in the face of uncertainty. It's about creating a foundation for authentic leadership, one where fear no longer paralyzes but empowers.

Vision and inheritance

A leader's vision is their North Star, guiding every decision and action. But creating a compelling vision requires deep self-reflection. *What are your values? What do you stand for? What kind of legacy do you want to leave behind?* These are the fundamental questions that every leader must answer.

In my role as CEO, crafting a vision that was aligned with my personal values of love, courage, and excellence was essential. A vision that was deeply rooted in who I am as a person was not only more authentic, but it also felt easier to communicate to my team. When leaders are clear about their values and vision, they inspire others to buy into that vision. A leader's vision should reflect their true self, something that resonates on a personal level and connects with the hearts of those they lead.

Understanding the legacy

Leadership is never a blank slate. As a CEO, I inherited not just the role but also the history, culture, and values of the organization I was stepping into. Early in my tenure, I took time to reflect on the legacy I had inherited—the good and the bad. This process involved understanding the values that had shaped the organization and identifying areas where change was needed. Leaders who embrace this process of reflection honor the past while simultaneously charting a course for the future. Self-reflection allows leaders to reconcile the legacy they've inherited with the legacy they hope to create.

The power of intention

Intention is the invisible force that propels successful leadership. Self-reflection helps leaders clarify their intentions, ensuring that every action taken aligns with their deeper purpose. My intention was always clear: to lead with authenticity, to create a culture where individuals could thrive, and to build something meaningful that would endure. When leaders are clear about their intentions, they inspire others to follow suit.

Mapping your strategy

A theory of action is more than a strategic plan—it's a road map that connects your vision with practical steps. This theory evolves through reflection on what matters most and how to achieve it. During my time as CEO, I have regularly revisited the organization's goals, aligning them with my vision and crafting strategies that are actionable and impactful. This process of reflection ensures that our strategy isn't just a document on a shelf—it's a living, breathing guide that evolves as we do.

Embracing self-awareness

Self-awareness is the glue that holds everything together. It enables leaders to navigate challenges with clarity, resilience, and grace. For me, this means regularly pausing to assess how I show up as a leader. *Am I acting in alignment with my values? Am I leading out of intention or reaction?* Cultivating self-awareness transformed my decision-making process, strengthening my ability to lead with integrity and confidence.

Conclusion

The practice of looking in the mirror is far more than a symbolic gesture; it is a powerful tool for transformative leadership. By embracing self-reflection, we can lead with authenticity, clarity, and intention. This practice has shaped how I lead, how I connect with others, and how I navigate the complexities of executive leadership. As we move forward, we'll explore how this internal work translates into building a high-performing leadership team and creating lasting impact.

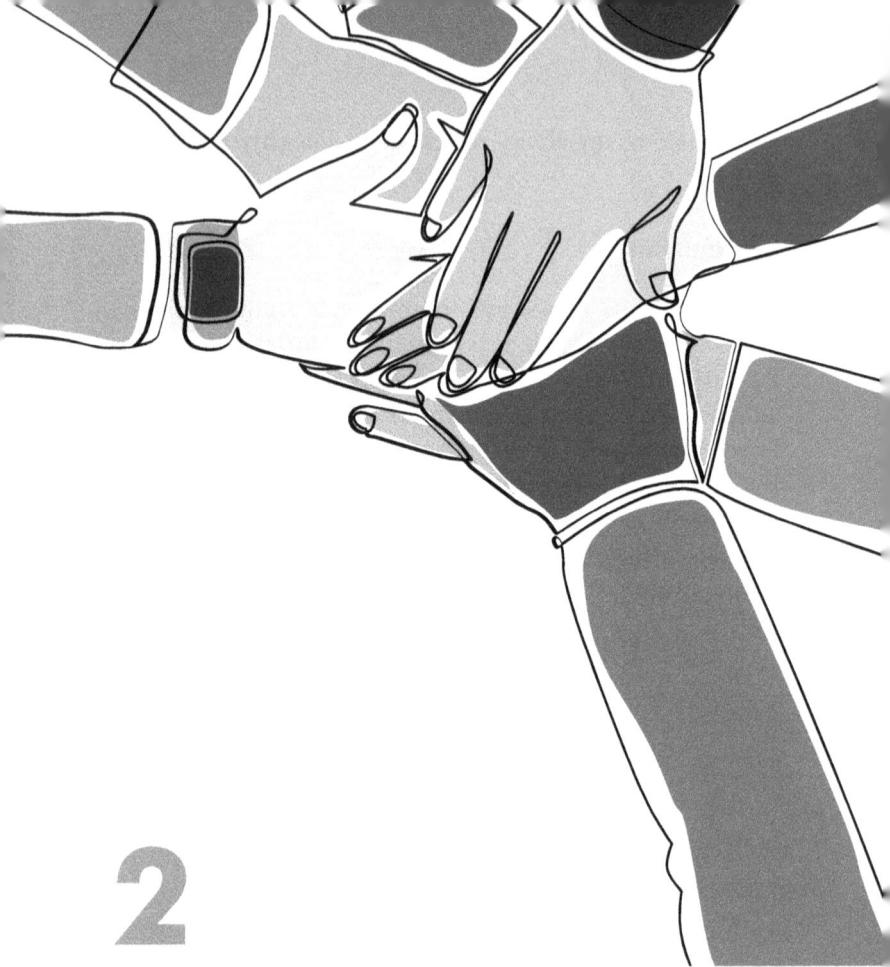

2

UNSWEEP UNDER THE RUG
– CLEANING UP THE CULTURE MESS

As a child, I had a deep affection for *Peanuts*, the beloved comic strip by Charles Schulz, and particularly for Charlie Brown and his quirky gang of friends. I always found myself drawn to the simplicity and honesty of their lives. Among them was Pig-Pen, the perpetually dusty character who seemed to carry with him a cloud of dirt and grime wherever he went. He was a peculiar character—always surrounded by a swirling cloud of dust, no matter where he went or how hard he tried to escape it. I remember being both fascinated and perplexed by him. Why couldn't he seem to clean up? Why did the dust follow him so persistently, no matter where he went or how hard he tried to escape it? As a child, it seemed like a funny, albeit strange, quirk of a cartoon character. I couldn't understand how someone could be so oblivious to their perpetual mess. But looking back now, especially through the lens of my experiences as a leader, I find myself resonating with Pig-Pen in ways I never imagined. As it turns out, I, too, would come to understand the metaphor of constantly carrying around a mess that you don't always know how to deal with.

Leadership, especially at the executive level, often requires stepping into environments where that very same cloud of swirling dust exists. It's the "dirt" of unresolved conflicts, long-held frustrations, unspoken tensions, and cultural misalignment that we tend to ignore, sweep under the rug, or overlook. But no matter how much we try to avoid it, the mess doesn't go away. Instead, it follows us, clinging to the teams we lead, hindering their progress, dimming their potential, and, ultimately, threatening their success. This chapter explores the challenging but necessary work of *unsweeping* what has been shoved under the rug—and how leaders can navigate the tough terrain of team transformation in the process. It's a process that, while uncomfortable, is essential for any leader seeking to build a healthy, aligned, and high-performing team.

The importance of cleaning up the culture

Imagine trying to cook a beautiful, elaborate meal in a kitchen where the counters are covered in crumbs, dirty dishes fill the sink, and the trash has spilled over onto the floor. It's not only unpleasant—it's nearly impossible to create something nourishing in such a chaotic environment. In fact, trying to work in that environment could feel utterly defeating, as though no matter how much you try, you are constantly fighting against an underlying mess that threatens to overwhelm you. Similarly, a leadership team that is surrounded by unresolved issues, hidden conflicts, and cultural misalignments cannot thrive, no matter how talented or dedicated its members are. A cluttered, toxic, or fragmented culture is a barrier to success, innovation, and sustainable performance. And no matter how hard you try to push forward, that mess will continue to undermine your efforts.

When I took on the role of CEO, I inherited a talented team with a long-standing reputation for making a meaningful impact in the community. They had achieved incredible things, and there was no shortage of potential. But beneath the surface, there were challenges—unspoken frustrations, unresolved conflicts, and a deep-seated weariness that had accumulated over the years from working in a high-stakes, high-pressure environment. Despite all the potential the team had, the organizational "kitchen" was in desperate need of a cleanup. Without addressing these underlying issues, it would have been impossible to take the next step toward greater achievement and deeper collaboration.

Acknowledging this cultural clutter wasn't easy. It required me to confront an uncomfortable truth: Leadership teams are often complicit in creating or tolerating the mess. Whether through avoidance, a lack of clarity, or a failure to address conflict head-on, leaders can unintentionally contribute to the cultural clutter. Many of us don't want to rock the boat, so we ignore things, brush issues aside, or hope that they'll resolve themselves. But what I quickly learned, and what I had to come to terms with, was this: If you avoid the mess long enough, it doesn't just go away. In fact, it only grows. However, as I came to understand, the first step toward real transformation is not ignoring the mess but *owning* it—no matter how uncomfortable, inconvenient, or complex that may be. Without acknowledging it, we couldn't move forward as a team, and our potential would remain untapped.

Digging up the past

Cleaning up the culture often requires going back to the beginning—digging into the past, even when it's messy and painful. This isn't easy work, but it is essential if we want to build a foundation for the future. As a new CEO, I knew that in order to lead my team forward, I had to first address the unresolved issues and dynamics that had been left behind. This meant looking under the rug and confronting the difficult, sometimes hidden, aspects of the team's culture. Often, we'd prefer to keep the past buried, to gloss over it and move forward. But if you don't dig deep enough to examine the origins of your issues, you risk repeating the same mistakes or perpetuating the same toxic behaviors.

When we began this process, it felt as though we were unearthing layers of dust and debris that had accumulated over time. Long-buried hurts came to the surface, frustrations were voiced for the first time, and unspoken tensions were revealed. It felt uncomfortable, like peeling back layers of wallpaper only to discover rot underneath. The feelings that emerged were raw, and the issues we had to address were often difficult to face. But this process, while painful, was also absolutely necessary. We had to look honestly at what was going on beneath the surface in order to understand why the team was struggling to function at its best.

To lead through this transformation, I had to confront the organizational culture I inherited—both its strengths and its challenges. While I was not at the helm when the long-standing culture issues brewed, I understood that as CEO, it was now my responsibility to own them. It was my job to address the clutter, tackle the uncomfortable truths, and guide our team through the process of realignment and renewal. This required vulnerability—not to admit personal fault, but to acknowledge the reality we faced and commit to fixing it together. I reminded myself—and the team—that the purpose of this "excavation" was not to assign blame but to create a deeper understanding of the forces that had shaped our current reality. Only through this understanding could we hope to move forward in a healthier, more productive way.

Confronting the cultural mess

Once we began peeling back the layers of tension and unresolved issues, we were faced with the daunting task of confronting them directly. This phase of transformation is much like cleaning out a cluttered garage: Everything has to come out before you can decide what to keep, what to fix, and what to discard. There's no way around it. The process is messy, emotional, and often overwhelming. In fact, it's hard to make sense of everything all at once, and it can feel like you're simply making more of a mess. But this messy phase is essential if you want to create something stronger, clearer, and more aligned.

As leaders, we tend to shy away from this level of confrontation. It's uncomfortable, and it can feel like opening Pandora's box. For my team, this process meant long, heated discussions, emotional outbursts, and confronting uncomfortable truths. People aired grievances they had held back for years, and at times, the atmosphere was thick with tension. There were moments when it felt like the walls were closing in, and it seemed easier to simply walk away from the conversation altogether. But what I learned during this phase is that avoiding these conversations only delays the inevitable. The mess doesn't simply disappear—it festers. It becomes a ticking time bomb, ready to explode at any moment. Ignoring the elephant in the room only makes it harder to move forward.

By bringing these issues to the surface, we created space for honest, real dialogue. We were able to ask difficult, probing questions:

- What's working well, and what isn't?

- Where have we failed each other?

- What do we need to heal in order to move forward?

The more we dug into these questions, the more we understood how deeply these unaddressed issues had impacted our culture and our performance. But the more we faced them head-on, the more empowered we became to make changes. It wasn't easy, but it was worth it.

Seeking outside facilitation

At a certain point during our cleanup, the mess felt too overwhelming to tackle on our own. After a particularly heated meeting where tensions reached a boiling point, I realized that we needed external support—a neutral third party who could guide us through the most challenging parts of this transformation. The facilitators would not only help us sort through the mess but also act as a mirror, reflecting our behaviors and patterns without the emotional charge we had all accumulated.

Bringing in an outside facilitator turned out to be one of the best decisions I made during this process. A facilitator brought a fresh, impartial perspective to the table. They helped us reframe conflicts, uncover deeper issues, and identify pathways toward resolution. With their help, we were able to see the patterns in our behavior and confront them in a constructive way. Without the facilitator, it would have been too easy for us to fall back into old patterns of behavior.

Having a facilitator also allowed me, as CEO, to step back from the role of "leader" and become a participant in the process. I wasn't just orchestrating the change—I was actively involved in it. This level of shared participation was crucial in building trust. Leaders must model the openness and vulnerability they ask of their teams. I had to show that I was willing to be just as vulnerable and open to criticism as anyone else. Having a facilitator made it possible for me to be more authentic in my own process of transformation, which encouraged the same from the team.

The grit and grace of transformation

Transformation is never a smooth or linear path. It requires grit—the determination to push through the tough moments—and grace—the ability to hold space for healing and growth. There were times during our journey when it would have been easier to give up, to settle for "good enough" rather than continuing to push for true alignment. We could have stopped and said, "This is fine. We've done enough." But that's not what leadership is about.

My team showed remarkable resilience. We committed to honest dialogue, even when it felt uncomfortable or emotionally taxing. We practiced active listening, trying to understand each other's perspectives without judgment. And we held one another accountable, not from a place of blame but from a shared commitment to growth and mutual respect. We knew that we were in this together, and that commitment helped us push through the hard times.

Ultimately, this process wasn't just about addressing the issues of the past—it was about creating a stronger foundation for the future. We clarified our shared values, defined our expectations, and set clear norms for how we would work together moving forward. We knew that the cultural cleanup wasn't just about getting rid of the mess—it was about building something stronger, more cohesive, and more aligned for the long term.

The beauty of alignment

Three years after embarking on this journey of culture transformation, the results were unmistakable. Our executive leadership team had shed the weight of unresolved issues, and we were now operating as a cohesive, aligned unit. We were connected not just by our work but by a shared purpose, vision, and set of values. There was an energy in the air that hadn't been there before—one of collaboration, trust, and mutual respect.

But the change didn't stop there. The impact rippled out across the organization. Teams communicated more effectively, trust deepened, and collaboration flourished. The hard, often uncomfortable work of cleaning up the cultural mess had paid off in ways that exceeded my expectations. We had built a team that was stronger, more resilient, and more capable than ever before.

Lessons for leaders

Cleaning up the culture is not a one-time event—it's an ongoing commitment. Below are the key lessons I learned throughout this process:

- **Acknowledge the mess**: Transformation begins with honesty. Don't ignore the signs of cultural misalignment. Address them head-on before they grow too large to ignore.

- **Create space for dialogue**: Encourage open, honest communication where team members feel safe expressing their thoughts and feelings.

- **Seek support when needed**: Don't hesitate to bring in external facilitation or expertise when the mess feels too overwhelming. It can make all the difference.

- **Lead with vulnerability**: Your willingness to be vulnerable as a leader sets the tone for the entire team. Show them that it's safe to open up and share their truth.

- **Stay the course**: Culture transformation takes time and persistence. Trust the process, even when it feels challenging or uncomfortable.

Conclusion

Just like Pig-Pen, every team carries its share of dust and debris. But unlike Pig-Pen, we don't have to live with it. By unsweeping what's been hidden under the rug and committing to the messy but necessary work of culture transformation, leaders can create teams that are not only effective but also deeply connected, resilient, and aligned.

The journey may be messy, but the outcome is worth it: a team that operates from a place of truth, trust, and shared purpose. The work of cleaning up the culture isn't just about fixing what's broken—it's about creating a foundation for something extraordinary.

3

IT'S VEGAS, BABY!
– CRAFTING A DETAILED BLUEPRINT FOR ORGANIZATIONAL SUCCESS

I recently had the chance to visit the Cosmopolitan in Las Vegas, and I have to say, the experience was nothing short of dazzling. Bright lights flashed from every corner of the casino, the sounds of slot machines played in the background, and the delicious smell of decadent food wafted through the air, teasing my senses. It was an overwhelming, sensory-rich environment designed to immerse you in the experience. My mission, as straightforward as it seemed, was simple: find my sister, who had texted me that she was somewhere near a particular restaurant. "Easy enough," I thought, pulling out my phone and heading toward the location she'd mentioned. I felt confident—until I actually stepped inside.

The moment I entered the casino's labyrinthine halls, I found myself quickly lost. I tried to follow the directions she'd sent me, but the more I walked, the more I realized that every hallway, every sign, and every flashing light was leading me in circles. I was getting nowhere. It felt like I was in an endless maze, unable to move forward, distracted by the flashing lights, the slot machines, and the general chaos of the place. The more I looked for my sister, the more I realized I wasn't just wandering; I was becoming increasingly overwhelmed.

What I didn't realize in that moment, but certainly understood later, was that the casino had been designed this way *on purpose*. Every hallway, every sign, every flicker of light had been strategically placed to keep me engaged, keep me wandering, and, most importantly, keep me spending money. The mazelike layout wasn't a coincidence. The architects of that space had a very clear vision of what they wanted me to experience, and they had used every element of design to achieve it. This wasn't just a building—it was an immersive, intentional environment built to guide and shape behavior without the visitor even realizing it.

Eventually, I did find my sister. But that experience, disorienting as it was, left me with an unexpected leadership lesson: Without a clear road map or a defined set of expectations, people get lost. If CEOs and organizational leaders fail to design and communicate a vision with purpose, their teams will wander aimlessly, distracted by their own priorities, uncertain of their direction, and ultimately uncertain of how to move forward. This chapter is about creating a clear and purposeful blueprint for your organization—what I call a road map that not only guides your people but also enables them to succeed in a more structured and intentional way.

The power of clarity

At its core, leadership is all about alignment. It's about ensuring that everyone in the organization, from your senior leadership team to the newest hire, understands what success looks like and how to achieve it. Yet, despite how essential this alignment is, many leaders often underestimate the importance of setting and communicating clear expectations. Too often, we assume that our team *just gets it*. We believe that if we have a quick conversation about our goals, that will be enough, and the team will follow. But in reality, that assumption couldn't be further from the truth.

The reality is this: *unclear expectations create chaos*. When expectations are not crystal clear, people will interpret their roles in different ways. Their priorities will diverge, and team performance will suffer. Think about it: Imagine trying to navigate a city with no street signs, no maps, and no GPS system to guide you. The confusion would be palpable, and the progress would be frustratingly slow. You'd probably feel like you're spinning your wheels, unsure of where you're headed or how to get where you want to go.

In organizations, the same principle holds true. When leadership fails to clearly articulate a vision or a road map, misunderstandings take root, and people operate in silos, unsure of how their work connects to the larger mission or strategy. However, when expectations are set clearly and communicated with precision, those expectations act as a well-lit path, empowering teams to move forward with clarity, focus, and purpose.

Clarity drives results. It minimizes ambiguity, gives teams direction, and ensures alignment at every level of the organization. As a leader, when you are clear about what you expect—whether that's about team performance, personal development, or organizational objectives—your team will be empowered to exceed those expectations, often achieving far more than you ever imagined.

Lessons from unexpected places: Vegas and the power of intentional design

Las Vegas casinos are often regarded as some of the most meticulously designed spaces in the world. Every element of these spaces is carefully crafted with a specific outcome in mind. The placement of slot machines, the aroma of the air, the lack of windows, even the absence of clocks—these elements have all been intentionally designed to keep people engaged and encourage them to spend. Their goal is to create an immersive experience that subtly, but powerfully, guides people's behavior.

For leaders, the lesson here is clear and powerful: *design matters*. Just as the architects of Las Vegas casinos design experiences to produce specific behavioral outcomes, organizational leaders must intentionally design their vision to influence organizational behavior, culture, and success. Leadership isn't passive; it's about actively shaping an environment that aligns with the desired outcomes.

Think about it this way:

- Every message you share with your team,

- Every decision you make as a leader,

- Every process you implement within your organization,

… all of these things communicate something about your vision and expectations. So, ask yourself: *Is it clear? Is it aligned? Does it inspire action?*

When crafting your organizational blueprint, it's important to ask yourself deeper questions:

- What experience do I want my team to have on a daily basis?

- What behaviors do I want to encourage within my team or organization?

- What outcomes do I expect from my team, and how will we measure success?

Leaders simply can't afford to leave these things to chance. Just as the architects of Las Vegas designed a total sensory experience with great care and foresight, as a leader, you must ensure that every detail of your organizational design is aligned with your vision. Every interaction, every message, and every process should help move you closer to your goals.

Think, ink, articulate: turning vision into tangible action

Having a vision in your mind isn't enough. For your vision to be meaningful and have an impact, it must be documented, communicated, and reinforced consistently. This is where the process of think, ink, and articulate comes into play—an approach that helps turn abstract ideas into concrete actions that can guide your team.

1. **Think**: Start with deep reflection and intention.

   - What is your vision for your team and your organization? What does success look like for you?

   - What core values will guide your decisions and actions?

   - What expectations do you have for yourself, for your team, and for the organization as a whole?

For me, this step often required carving out some quiet time away from the hustle and bustle of daily work—time to think, reflect, and write down my thoughts. This step of mental clarity and focus is essential. I wrote down my thoughts and then refined them, slowly clarifying what mattered most to me as a leader and what I wanted to achieve. The clearer I became internally about my own expectations, the easier it was to communicate those expectations externally to my team.

2. **Ink**: Once you have clarity about your vision, it's time to put it into writing. A vision that isn't documented is simply a fleeting thought—something that's easily forgotten or overlooked.

   - Create a compelling mission statement that captures the essence of your vision.

   - Develop a visual representation of your core values so that your team can easily connect with them.

   - Lay out an actionable road map with clear milestones, goals, and objectives to help track progress.

Putting these elements into writing makes them real—it transforms an abstract vision into a tangible set of guiding principles that can influence decision-making, behavior, and organizational culture.

3. **Articulate:** Communication is critical to success. Your vision must be communicated clearly, consistently, and authentically.

   - Share your vision in every setting possible—whether it's in meetings, emails, or strategy sessions.

   - Reinforce your vision during one-on-ones with team members and during team check-ins.

   - Celebrate successes that align with the vision, and address any deviations constructively.

Consistency is key here. One single declaration of your vision won't cut it. People need to hear it, see it, and feel it repeatedly. The more often you articulate and reinforce your expectations, the more deeply ingrained those expectations will become in the culture. Your team will not only understand them but will begin to embody them in their work.

Navigating transition

Change is inevitable in any organization. Team members come and go, roles evolve, and priorities shift. During periods of transition, your vision becomes even more important. It becomes your anchor—a constant, a North Star—that keeps you and your team grounded and moving forward.

When I first took on the role of CEO, I quickly realized that turnover was one of the most disruptive challenges I would face. Every new hire brought fresh perspectives, new energy, and new ideas—but also uncertainty and the need for adjustment. The question I had to answer was: *How do we ensure continuity of culture and expectations during these times of transition?*

The answer lies in the clarity of your vision. When expectations are documented, reinforced, and universally understood, transitions become much smoother. New team members can quickly align with the organizational culture and objectives because the road map is already in place. Instead of chaos and confusion, there is continuity and alignment.

Keeping the vision alive

Finally, once your vision is articulated, it must be communicated regularly and with purpose. If clarity is the foundation of success, communication is the vehicle that drives it forward. But communication isn't just about words—it's about actions. As a leader, you must model the behaviors you expect from your team.

Conclusion

Just as the architects of Las Vegas casinos design immersive, intentional experiences, leaders must craft a vision and set expectations with precision and thoughtfulness. Clarity is the cornerstone of organizational success, and it begins with you.

By thinking deeply, documenting intentionally, and communicating consistently, you create a blueprint that aligns your team toward a common goal. When you do this, you eliminate confusion, build trust, and inspire your team to achieve extraordinary outcomes.

If my experience in that Las Vegas casino taught me anything, it's this: Wandering aimlessly might be fine for tourists, but it's disastrous for teams. Your job as a leader is to provide the road map—clear, intentional, and inspiring—so your team can find its way, together.

It's Vegas, baby—let's design the leadership team experience that drives success.

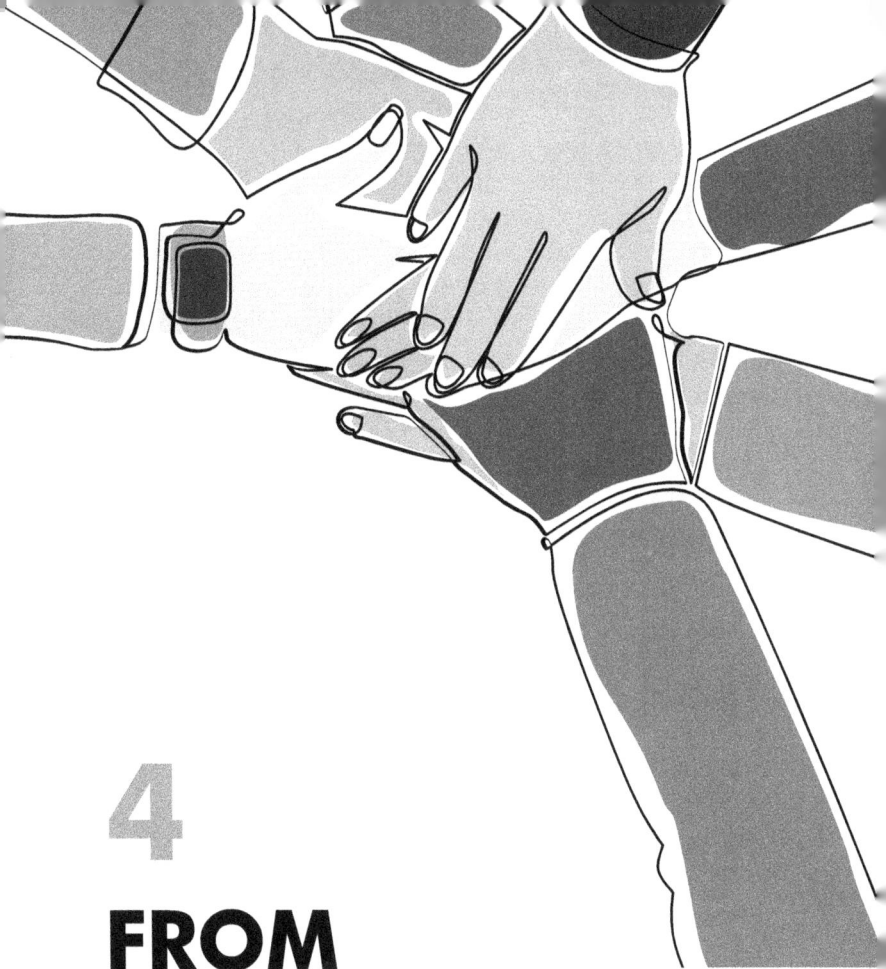

4

FROM CLASSROOM TO BOARDROOM
– TEACHING AS A LEADERSHIP SUPERPOWER

In my first year as a teacher, my classroom was small but vibrant. It was a place of both challenge and opportunity. I stood in front of twenty eager faces every day, each student ready to learn and grow. It wasn't just about imparting knowledge; I had a deeper responsibility. I had to inspire confidence in my students, ignite their curiosity, and build trust with them. It was essential that they believed in themselves and their potential, that they understood they could achieve greatness, not just in their academic accomplishments but in life. Teaching was about connection—not merely the delivery of lessons. It was about fostering an environment where each child felt seen, heard, and encouraged to excel.

Years later, as I transitioned into the role of a CEO, I came to an important realization: I am still a teacher. The only difference is that my classroom has grown significantly. My role now extends beyond twenty students to encompass a much larger, more diverse audience—staff, executive leaders, families, and students. But the core principles of teaching still apply. My job has evolved, but the foundational work of a teacher remains at the heart of it. Instead of teaching math or science, my job is to impart a vision. Instead of guiding individual students, I now inspire teams. And rather than cultivating academic excellence, I focus on building a culture where every person understands their role in achieving greatness as a collective.

The principles of teaching are far more applicable to leadership than many realize. The best teachers don't merely disseminate information—they model core values, create clarity, spark engagement, and build an environment where learning is continuous and growth is encouraged. As a CEO, I discovered that my leadership truly transformed when I embraced my role as a teacher—guiding my organization through intentional instruction, vision, and mentorship.

This chapter will explore how CEOs can step into the role of master teachers—nurturing organizational growth, aligning teams around a common purpose, and empowering individuals to excel. It's not just about being a boss; it's about becoming a teacher who empowers others to lead.

The CEO as the chief visionary officer

Great teachers always begin with a clear sense of purpose. They understand the broader objective and know exactly what their students need to learn, why it matters, and how to guide them toward mastery. Similarly, as a CEO, you must start with a vision. As the chief visionary officer, you are responsible for designing the entire learning journey for your organization. Your vision is not simply a set of goals or strategies—it's the curriculum that informs every decision you make, guides every interaction, and influences every outcome. It's the bedrock upon which the organization's culture is built.

Visionary leadership goes beyond setting financial or operational goals. It shapes culture by answering three essential questions:

1. **Where are we going?** This is the destination. It's the end goal, the vision for what the organization will look like when it has achieved success.

2. **Why does it matter?** This is the purpose. It's the deeper *why* behind the vision—the reason the organization exists and why the work matters to everyone involved.

3. **How will we get there?** This is the plan. It's the road map, the strategy, and the actionable steps that will move the organization forward, turning vision into reality.

When these questions are answered clearly and consistently, they provide a framework that helps guide every decision, action, and interaction within the organization. In teaching terms, this is your "lesson plan" for the organization—a structured guide that sets the tone for the entire educational journey of your team, aligning them with the overarching vision and ensuring continuous growth. As a CEO, your vision is not something that can be static or vague; it must be an active, evolving curriculum that guides your team toward success.

Drawing parallels between teaching and leadership

Teaching and leadership have far more in common than many realize. Both roles require the ability to guide, influence, and inspire others. While the context might differ—classroom versus boardroom—the fundamental principles of effective leadership are deeply rooted in the art of teaching. Here are a few key parallels:

- **Clarity**: Just as teachers break down complex concepts into digestible lessons, effective leaders clarify organizational goals into actionable steps. In teaching, a teacher's ability to simplify abstract ideas and present them in a way that's easy to understand is crucial to student success. Similarly, as a leader, you must translate the organization's broad vision into clear, actionable strategies. Every person must understand what success looks like and how they contribute to achieving it.

- **Engagement**: Teachers excel at inspiring curiosity and fostering active participation in their students. Great teachers don't just talk; they engage students in ways that spark their interest and encourage them to take ownership of their learning. As a CEO, you must do the same for your team. Leaders must foster an environment of buy-in and collective ownership, where team members feel personally invested in the greater organization's mission and success.

- **Accountability**: Teachers set clear expectations for success and hold students accountable for their progress. Similarly, leaders must ensure accountability within their teams. Whether it's meeting deadlines, maintaining a positive work culture, or hitting performance milestones, clear expectations and accountability are vital. As a leader, you set the standards, but it's the team that must rise to meet them.

Both roles require patience, empathy, and authenticity. Effective teachers meet students where they are and guide them toward where they need to be. As a CEO, this means understanding your team's strengths and areas for growth, and providing the support, guidance, and resources they need to succeed. The most effective leaders don't dictate—they teach, mentor, and support.

Crafting the "curriculum"

A successful teacher doesn't simply walk into a classroom and start talking off the cuff. They craft lesson plans, map out learning objectives, and design meaningful experiences to ensure their students achieve success. Similarly, as a CEO, you must adopt the same level of intentionality when creating your leadership "curriculum."

Here's how you can design your blueprint for organizational learning and growth:

1. **Define key teachings**: What are the core principles and values you want your team to learn and embody? These might include:

   + Your organizational vision and mission, clearly defined and easily understood.

   + Expectations for behavior, communication, and accountability. This sets the foundation for how individuals will interact with one another, how they will align their actions with company values, and how they will take responsibility for their roles.

+ The specific skills and mindset required for success. This is not just about technical know-how, but about cultivating qualities like resilience, adaptability, creativity, and collaboration.

2. **Align lessons with strategy**: Every teaching moment must tie into the bigger picture of your strategy. If innovation is a core value, create lessons that inspire creativity and risk-taking. If teamwork and collaboration are key to your success, provide lessons that teach how to work effectively across boundaries and leverage collective strengths.

3. **Use storytelling**: Stories are an incredibly powerful tool for teaching. They make abstract ideas relatable, emotional, and memorable. As a CEO, your personal experiences—your successes, failures, and moments of clarity—become invaluable teaching tools. These stories reinforce the *why* behind your vision and provide real-world examples that show how abstract concepts can be applied in practice.

4. **Create artifacts**: Just as teachers use handouts, worksheets, and other resources to help students grasp concepts, as a CEO, you can create tangible artifacts to reinforce your teachings. These might include visual diagrams, written handbooks, or strategic road maps that your team can refer back to. These documents serve as reminders of what's important and help keep the learning process consistent throughout the organization.

When your curriculum is clear, structured, and accessible, your team not only understands the goals but also the specific skills and behaviors required to achieve them. This helps them stay focused and aligned with the vision.

Teaching methods and strategies

Even the best curriculum will fall short if it's not communicated effectively. In teaching, methods matter. Just like a teacher uses various methods to deliver lessons—lectures, visuals, group work, and feedback—a CEO must diversify their communication strategies to ensure the vision reaches everyone in ways that are clear, impactful, and engaging.

Here are some key teaching strategies for CEOs:

- **Multichannel communication**: Just as teachers use a variety of methods—lectures, visuals, group work, and feedback—to engage their students, CEOs must use a mix of communication channels. This might include:

  - All-hands meetings to communicate vision and progress.

  - Smaller group discussions for deeper dialogue and questions.

  - Written communication such as emails, newsletters, and reports to reinforce key points.

  - One-on-one sessions to offer personalized feedback and address specific challenges.

- **Repetition with variation**: The best teachers don't just say things once and expect students to understand. They repeat core concepts in different ways, using examples, stories, and analogies to reinforce learning. As a CEO, repetition is essential. Share your vision and expectations consistently, but do so in new and engaging ways. Tell fresh stories, provide new examples, and continuously bring the vision to life in diverse formats to keep your team engaged.

- **Foster a culture of feedback**: Teaching isn't a one-way street. The best teachers listen to their students, assess their understanding, and adapt their approach accordingly. Similarly, as a CEO, you must create a culture where feedback flows in all directions. Regularly ask your team:

  - "What do you understand about our vision and expectations?"

  - "Where do you feel unclear?"

  - "How can I better support your growth?"

Feedback is invaluable for refining your message, ensuring alignment, and helping your team continuously learn and evolve with you.

- **Celebrate learning and progress**: Just as teachers celebrate their students' achievements—whether it's mastering a concept, improving a skill, or overcoming a challenge—you, too, must celebrate your team's successes. Recognition reinforces the lessons you're teaching and motivates people to stay committed to the journey. Whether it's a small win or a major milestone, celebrating progress keeps morale high and encourages continued effort.

Leading by example

The most powerful teaching tool a leader possesses is their own behavior. People don't learn just by listening to what you say—they learn from what you do. As a CEO, it's essential that you embody the values, principles, and vision you want your team to adopt. You are the living example of the culture you wish to build.

- **Be authentic**: Your team can spot inconsistency from a mile away. If you expect accountability, hold yourself accountable first. Align your actions with your words, and lead with transparency. When you demonstrate authenticity, it inspires trust and fosters a deeper connection with your team.

- **Model core values**: The best leaders don't just talk about values—they live them. If collaboration is a priority, actively work across teams. If courage is essential, demonstrate it in your decisions. When you embody the values you expect from your team, it encourages them to follow suit.

- **Encourage open dialogue**: Foster an environment where questions are welcomed, curiosity is encouraged, and collaboration thrives. When you model openness and vulnerability, it gives your team permission to do the same. Open dialogue fosters a culture of innovation and continuous improvement.

Empowering other leaders as teachers

Teaching doesn't stop with the CEO. In thriving organizations, leadership is shared at all levels. As CEO, your job is to empower others to become teachers in their own right. By developing and nurturing internal leaders, you extend the impact of your vision and build a culture of mentorship.

- **Develop internal leaders**: Identify individuals within your organization who can help carry the vision forward. Equip them with the tools, confidence, and opportunities to teach and inspire their own teams. When leaders at every level embrace the role of teacher, they become agents of transformation.

- **Monitor progress and adapt**: Just as teachers regularly assess their students' learning, CEOs must monitor how well the organization is embracing the vision. Track progress, celebrate wins, and adjust strategies as needed to ensure alignment and continuous growth.

- **Create a learning culture**: Encourage continuous growth by fostering curiosity, reflection, and innovation. Challenges become learning opportunities, and success is celebrated not just for the outcomes but for the process of growth itself.

Conclusion

At its heart, leadership is teaching. It's about articulating a clear vision, guiding people toward shared goals, and creating an environment where growth, learning, and transformation can occur. Just as great teachers inspire their students to see their own potential, visionary CEOs empower their teams to achieve new heights.

By crafting a clear "curriculum," delivering it with purpose, and leading by example, you will transform your organization into a thriving learning community. And when leaders at every level embrace the role of teacher, the organization evolves into something extraordinary—resilient, aligned, and poised for success.

My classroom may have grown, but my purpose remains the same: to teach, inspire, and equip others to excel. This is the power of leadership as teaching—a masterclass in building a culture of clarity, growth, and visionary guidance.

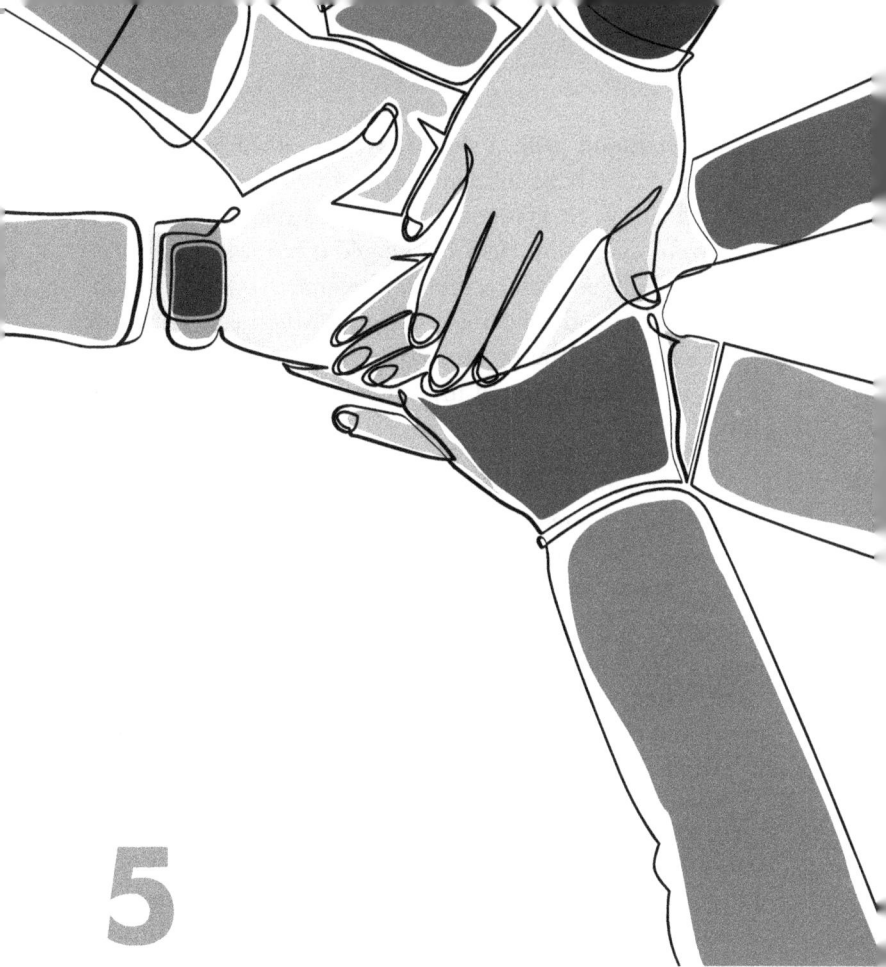

5

ELBOW TO ELBOW
– EMBRACING SIDE-BY-SIDE COACHING

One afternoon, with a shared sweet tooth prompting us, I set out to bake brownies with my two sons. The task seemed simple at first—just mix the batter, pour it into a pan, bake, and enjoy. How hard could it be? But what I experienced in that kitchen that day became a powerful lesson in leadership and coaching—one that would stay with me for a long time. The process was not as straightforward as I had imagined. It tested my patience, understanding, and ability to lead.

As we began, my sons eagerly declared, "We can do it ourselves!" They wanted the freedom to try things on their own. At first, I admired their enthusiasm. But quickly, I realized that each step in the process required guidance. The measurements had to be precise, and I needed to show them how to mix the ingredients without splattering batter everywhere. Then, when it came time to pour the mixture into the pan, I had to demonstrate how to do so evenly, ensuring the brownies would bake uniformly.

As we moved through each step, I saw moments of frustration on their faces. There were times when they wanted to give up, feeling the process was much harder than it appeared. But other times, I could see their determination. They needed encouragement, a simple "You're doing great! Keep going," to help them push through their frustration. At these moments, I reminded myself that this experience wasn't about me doing it for them. It wasn't about giving orders or taking over the process. It was about guiding them, elbow to elbow, through the mess, the missteps, and, ultimately, the triumphs.

By the end, when we tasted the brownies together, their smiles were worth every bit of effort. They hadn't just created something delicious; they had learned skills they could apply next time. The experience had been messy, challenging, and full of mistakes, but it also had been incredibly rewarding.

This moment in the kitchen became a powerful metaphor for leadership through coaching. Just like my sons didn't need me to take over the task, teams don't need a CEO to fix everything for them. They need a leader to walk beside them—someone who can guide them, step in when necessary, offer feedback, and celebrate progress. True coaching requires patience, presence, and a deep understanding that growth doesn't happen through commands, but through collaboration. It's about walking alongside others, fostering their independence while offering the right amount of guidance and support.

This chapter explores how CEOs can embrace coaching as a core leadership practice, shifting from traditional "top-down" models to one that's grounded in trust, partnership, and side-by-side guidance.

Coaching as a modern leadership imperative

The concept of coaching has its origins in the Latin word *coche*, meaning "by or side by side." This etymology perfectly captures the essence of true coaching—it's not about instructing or directing from above, but about walking alongside someone, guiding them as they learn and grow. Coaching is a shared journey, where both the coach and the coachee learn from each other.

In today's rapidly changing organizational landscape, the role of CEOs has evolved significantly. The traditional hierarchical leadership model—where the CEO simply issues commands and delegates tasks—no longer suffices. The world has changed, and leadership needs to adapt. Successful leaders are now embracing a more collaborative approach, one in which coaching becomes a cornerstone of organizational growth and success. This shift represents a profound change in how we view leadership: it's no longer about power over others but about partnership and empowerment.

Coaching as a leadership practice empowers teams to build skills, solve problems, and reach their full potential. It transforms organizations from static, dependent entities into dynamic, learning-oriented communities capable of innovation and adaptability. When leaders embrace coaching, they create an environment that fosters learning, growth, and collaboration—key ingredients for success in today's fast-paced, ever-changing business world. Coaching is not just a tool—it is a mindset, a commitment to being present, to listening, and to guiding others as they reach new heights.

Understanding the core principles of true coaching

1. Studying together

Great leaders are not distant experts on high pedestals; they are co-learners, walking alongside their teams every step of the way. Just as a teacher learns alongside their students, a CEO must be willing to learn alongside their team. Effective coaching is about more than offering advice or instructions; it's about immersing yourself in the learning process. It's about engaging with your team's challenges, celebrating their successes, and growing together.

When CEOs embrace the learning process themselves, it fosters a shared sense of purpose. Teams see that their leader isn't merely directing them from afar but is actively involved in their development. This humility and willingness to learn alongside others not only strengthens trust but also sets a powerful example of continuous growth. It signals that growth is a lifelong endeavor and that no one, not even the CEO, is exempt from learning.

Practical strategies:

- **Participate in leadership workshops or team trainings with your staff.** This shows that you, too, are committed to growth. It also levels the playing field, allowing you to connect with your team on a deeper, more personal level.

- **Host book clubs or learning sessions where everyone discusses ideas together.** This fosters a culture of continuous learning, where everyone is encouraged to explore new ideas and share their insights.

- **Show curiosity during problem-solving.** Instead of assuming you have all the answers, ask questions, explore different perspectives, and invite your team to think through solutions with you.

When you learn alongside your team, you send a message that learning and growth are not top-down commands— they are collaborative efforts that everyone participates in.

2. Celebrating success

True coaching isn't just about correcting mistakes—it's also about recognizing and celebrating what's going well. Acknowledging success, both big and small, fuels morale and motivates individuals to keep going. Appreciation tells people, "I see you. I value your work, and I recognize your contribution." It reinforces the behaviors and actions that drive progress and helps build a sense of pride and ownership in the work being done.

As CEOs, celebrating success doesn't have to be elaborate or expensive. It can be as simple as a handwritten note of thanks, a public shout-out at a meeting, or a team lunch to celebrate a recent milestone. What matters most is the sincerity behind the acknowledgment. People want to feel that their hard work is seen and appreciated.

Key tip: Celebrate not just the outcomes, but also the effort and progress. When people see their hard work and persistence recognized, it reinforces their commitment to continuous improvement. Even when outcomes aren't perfect, recognizing the effort creates a culture where learning from mistakes is valued just as much as achieving success.

3. Intervention and support

Coaching requires timely intervention. Just as I stepped in when my sons' brownie batter needed extra mixing, CEOs must be attuned to when a team member or project is off course and needs support. However, intervention in coaching isn't about assigning blame—rather, it focuses on offering guidance, asking the right questions, and helping individuals navigate through challenges. The goal isn't to take over but to provide the resources and direction that will empower them to get back on track.

Practical strategies:

- **Watch for early warning signs of struggle.** These might include missed deadlines, unclear communication, or growing team tension. Address these issues early to prevent them from escalating.

- **Approach intervention with curiosity.** Instead of saying, "What went wrong?" try asking, "How can I help?" This opens the door for a more collaborative, solution-oriented conversation.

- **Offer resources, tools, or mentorship.** Empower your team with what they need to course-correct. Whether it's additional training, access to experts, or simply a brainstorming session, providing support helps people regain confidence and keep moving forward.

4. Redirecting and course correction

Feedback is one of the most essential tools in a coach's tool kit. Meaningful coaching involves redirecting individuals with constructive, actionable feedback. The goal is not to criticize, but to help team members recognize areas for improvement and give them the tools they need to do better. Feedback should be seen as a gift—a way to guide people toward their highest potential.

Practical framework for feedback:

1. **State observations**: Be specific about what you've noticed. For example, instead of saying, "The project is behind," you might say, "I saw that the project fell behind schedule this week."

2. **Ask questions**: Understand their perspective. You might ask, "What challenges came up that we can address?" or "How did you approach this task, and what might have helped you overcome obstacles?"

3. **Provide actionable guidance**: Offer clear, practical solutions. You could suggest, "Next time, we might want to break the task into smaller chunks to stay on schedule," or ask for their ideas on how to solve the problem.

4. **End on encouragement**: Always end on a positive note, reinforcing your belief in their abilities. For instance, "I know you can get this back on track. Let's course correct."

By providing clear, actionable feedback that focuses on improvement rather than blame, you help your team members grow, learn, and succeed.

Trust and connection through coaching

1. Establishing trust

Trust is the foundation of effective coaching. Without trust, feedback just feels like criticism, interventions feel like micromanagemeCnt, and celebrations feel hollow. Teams need to know that their CEO has their best interests at heart and genuinely cares about their success.

To build trust, CEOs must be transparent, consistent, and genuine. People need to understand why you're offering feedback or stepping in to help. They need to know that your intentions are rooted in their growth and success. Additionally, trust is built over time through actions, not words. You must follow through on commitments, show reliability, and always be honest—even when it's difficult.

To build trust, demonstrate vulnerability. Share your own challenges, admit when you don't have all the answers, and show humility. When you model transparency and openness, your team will feel safe doing the same.

2. Developing emotional intelligence

Effective coaches are emotionally intelligent. They understand not only their own emotions but also those of others. This awareness enables them to respond with empathy, wisdom, and sensitivity. For CEOs, cultivating emotional intelligence is critical for building strong relationships and fostering a positive organizational culture.

Practical tips:

- **Practice self-awareness**: Recognize your emotional triggers and understand how they influence your behavior. This will help you stay composed, especially in challenging situations.

- **Demonstrate empathy**: Listen deeply to your team members' concerns and show that you understand their perspectives.

- **Manage relationships**: Handle conflicts calmly, resolve misunderstandings with care, and focus on fostering positive, productive connections.

Before giving feedback or coaching, take a moment to pause and ask, *"What does this person need from me emotionally right now? Do they need encouragement, understanding, or clarity?"*

3. Creating a culture of learning

Coaching is not a one-off activity; it is a mindset embedded in the organizational culture. When CEOs prioritize coaching, they create an environment where learning, experimentation, and growth are celebrated. In such a culture, team members feel empowered to take risks, explore new ideas, and push the boundaries of what's possible.

How to foster a learning culture:

- **Normalize mistakes** as opportunities for growth. Encourage your team to see failure as a stepping stone rather than a setback.

- **Encourage curiosity** by asking reflective questions: "What did we learn from this?" or "How can we do this better next time?"

- **Invest in ongoing development** by providing access to training programs, mentorship opportunities, and leadership development initiatives.

Implementing coaching practices in the workplace

1. Coaching conversations

Effective coaching conversations are intentional, structured, and impactful. CEOs can use the following framework to guide these discussions:

1. **Set the context**: Begin by clarifying the purpose of the conversation and the desired outcome.

2. **Ask open-ended questions**: For example, "What's working well? What challenges are you facing?" This invites reflection and dialogue.

3. **Identify goals**: Collaborate on clear, actionable next steps to move forward.

4. **Hold accountable**: Follow up after the conversation to provide ongoing support and ensure progress.

2. Feedback mechanisms

Feedback is the engine of growth. CEOs must normalize feedback—both giving and receiving it—throughout the organization.

Best practices for feedback:

- **Give feedback promptly**—don't wait for annual reviews. Feedback is most effective when it's timely.

- **Be specific and constructive**. Avoid vague praise like "Good job." Instead, say something like, "Your detailed work on the project's timeline really helped us stay focused and on track."

- **Encourage upward feedback**. Ask your team, "How can I better support you?"

3. Measuring coaching impact

To ensure coaching drives results, leaders must evaluate its effectiveness. CEOs can:

- Use surveys or feedback tools to gauge team satisfaction and growth.

- Monitor key performance metrics that are tied to coaching outcomes.

- Reflect on team dynamics. Are trust and collaboration improving? Are goals being met?

By regularly measuring and adjusting coaching strategies, leaders can ensure that their coaching efforts are having a lasting, positive impact on the organization.

Conclusion

True coaching is not about standing above or behind your team. It's about walking alongside them, guiding them with intention, empathy, and unwavering support. Just as I stood side by side with my sons in the kitchen, teaching them how to bake brownies, CEOs must commit to guiding their teams through challenges, growth, and success.

When leaders embrace coaching as a core practice, they transform not only individuals but the entire organizational culture. Trust deepens, skills develop, and the team becomes more aligned and resilient. This is the power of holding hands—leading side by side toward a shared vision of success.

Leadership through coaching is not just a role; it's a gift. By guiding with candor and some patience, holding high expectations and belief, and celebrating progress, leaders empower their teams to rise to their full potential, one step at a time.

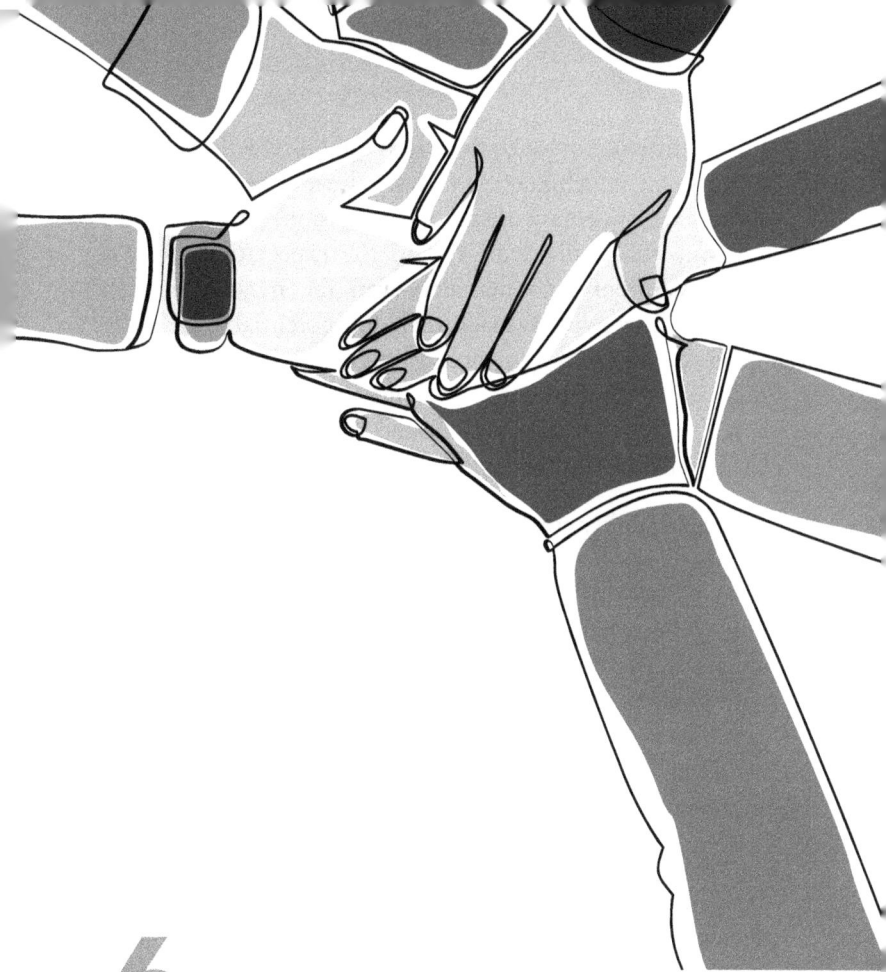

6

THE LITTLE
RED HEN
– TOUGH LOVE IS
STILL LOVE

I n any thriving organization, accountability is the foundation upon which success is built. Leadership is not just
about encouragement, inspiration, or vision—it's also about
ensuring that individuals rise to the expectations set for
them. Without accountability, even the most motivated
teams will struggle to reach their full potential. True leadership means holding people to high standards while also
supporting their growth. It's about ensuring that everyone
is accountable for their actions and responsibilities, and not
letting anyone slip through the cracks.

Accountability creates a culture of ownership and responsibility. It is what turns great ideas into tangible outcomes,
what transforms good intentions into measurable results.
This is especially important in high-performing teams
where excellence is the goal. Leaders are tasked not only
with guiding their teams but also ensuring they fulfill their
promises and commitments. Without this firm, yet supportive accountability, even the most capable individuals and
teams can falter.

One of my favorite stories growing up was *The Little Red
Hen*. In it, the Little Red Hen finds a grain of wheat and
decides to plant it. Along the way, she asks for help from
her friends—Dog, Cat, and Duck—at every step: planting,
harvesting, grinding the wheat, and baking the bread. Each
time, they refuse to help, saying, "Not I!" So, she does all
the work herself. When the bread is finally ready and smells
delicious, everyone wants to share the rewards. However, the
Little Red Hen holds them accountable for their lack of
effort and eats the bread herself.

The story is a simple yet powerful lesson in accountability.
The Little Red Hen did not allow anyone to take part in
the reward unless they were willing to put in the work. In
leadership, this story highlights the importance of fairness,
integrity, and the need to align effort with reward. If indi-

viduals are not held accountable for their contributions—or lack thereof—the result is resentment, disengagement, and inequity. The Little Red Hen's actions teach us that rewards should be earned, and when individuals fail to contribute, they forfeit their right to share in the success.

Early in my career, I was coached by an incredible guide who described the role of a leader as needing to "hold hands while holding feet to the fire." Leadership requires a delicate balance. As we guide with great belief and side-by-side support, as described in the previous chapter, we must also embrace the responsibility to hold our teammates to high standards. High-performing leaders understand the need to balance compassion with accountability. It's not enough to cheer from the sidelines or offer encouragement without also demanding results. In high-stakes environments, where success is often non-negotiable, accountability is the force that drives individuals and teams to deliver on their commitments. It is not about harsh punishment, but about reinforcing that expectations must be met. This chapter explores how leaders can effectively balance support with tough love, creating a culture where accountability inspires growth, excellence, and shared success.

Establishing clear expectations

The first step to accountability is clarity. Leaders cannot hold their team members accountable for expectations that were never properly communicated. It begins with a crystal-clear vision, one that connects individual roles to the success of the organization as a whole. When expectations are vague or undefined, accountability becomes impossible. Individuals may not know what success looks like or how to meet it, which can lead to frustration, confusion, and a lack of motivation. Therefore, it is the leader's responsibility to ensure that the vision is clear, achievable, and consistently reinforced.

A leader must ask themselves: What is the goal? What behaviors and performance standards will help us achieve it? Once those answers are defined, they must be shared with the team in an unambiguous manner. People perform best when they understand not only what is expected of them but also why their role is essential. A shared purpose motivates action. When individuals feel aligned with the organization's mission and understand the specific ways in which they contribute, they are more likely to be engaged and motivated.

Reinforcing the vision and goals: Expectations should align with the organizational vision. Goals set in previous chapters, such as team priorities and overarching objectives, should serve as the baseline for individual performance. For example, if the company's vision is to deliver "world-class customer service," then expectations for team members must be tied directly to this goal—whether through responsiveness, professionalism, or problem-solving. Every individual's daily actions should reflect and support the overarching vision. The alignment between individual behavior and organizational goals creates clarity and fosters a sense of collective purpose.

Communicating specific expectations: Generalities do not work. Instead of saying, "We need better customer service," a leader should communicate specifics: "All client emails must receive a reply within twenty-four hours," or "Resolve customer complaints within three business days." Specificity eliminates ambiguity and provides a measurable standard for success. Vague instructions or unclear expectations lead to confusion and unmet goals. The more specific and measurable the expectations, the easier it becomes to track progress and hold individuals accountable.

Linking responsibilities to organizational success: Every individual's work matters. Leaders should regularly remind team members how their responsibilities contribute to broader goals. A sales team member, for instance, needs to understand that hitting revenue targets enables the company to invest in employee development or expand into new markets. Connecting responsibilities to tangible outcomes builds a sense of purpose and accountability. It reminds individuals that their efforts are directly contributing to the success of the entire organization. This connection fosters ownership and reinforces that every action, no matter how small, plays a role in the company's larger success.

When expectations are clear, team members are empowered to rise to meet them. Ambiguity fosters confusion; clarity inspires confidence. With clear expectations in place, individuals know exactly what is expected of them and how their work aligns with the organization's goals.

Implementing accountability measures

Once expectations are in place, leaders must establish mechanisms to monitor progress and measure success. Accountability is not about micromanagement—it's about ensuring that performance aligns with what was promised. Leaders should create systems that allow for regular feedback, review, and assessment. Accountability measures should be viewed as tools for alignment, not punishment. They are designed to help individuals and teams stay on track and deliver the results they are capable of.

Developing metrics and key performance indicators (KPIs): Metrics provide objective, trackable ways to evaluate performance. Leaders should develop clear KPIs that reflect progress toward the organization's goals. For example, a marketing team might track conversion rates, campaign ROI, or social media engagement. A manufacturing team might measure units produced, error rates, or turnaround times. These metrics serve as tools for both recognition and improvement. By clearly defining measurable standards of success, leaders can assess progress and identify areas for improvement.

KPIs also create transparency within the team. When performance is tracked against clear benchmarks, team members can see how their individual efforts contribute to the larger picture. This fosters a culture of accountability where results are quantifiable and everyone is aware of their standing.

Conducting regular performance reviews: Feedback is the engine of accountability. Regular performance reviews allow leaders to assess progress, celebrate achievements, and address gaps before they widen. These reviews should be two-way conversations where leaders provide constructive input while also listening to team members' concerns and challenges. Performance reviews should not be limited to an annual event but should be ongoing and continuous. Regular check-ins provide a chance to address issues early, adjust strategies, and offer support where needed.

In addition to assessing performance, these reviews provide an opportunity to reinforce expectations and clarify any areas of uncertainty. A good performance review should not be about simply evaluating past actions but also about setting clear expectations for the future. This forward-looking approach helps individuals see where they are headed and what adjustments are necessary to reach their goals.

Addressing issues with constructive criticism: Leaders must be prepared to address underperformance or problematic behavior head-on. This requires delivering honest, clear, and actionable feedback. The key is to be firm yet fair. Instead of saying, "Your work has been disappointing," say, "I noticed that two recent projects missed deadlines. Let's explore what obstacles you're facing and how you can address them." Constructive criticism focuses on solutions rather than blame. Leaders should approach difficult conversations with courage, curiosity, and an open mind. The goal is not to criticize, but to help team members improve and succeed.

Accountability measures are not punishments; they are tools for alignment and growth. When implemented consistently, they keep individuals and teams on track toward excellence. Providing regular feedback and addressing issues as they arise ensures that individuals stay aligned with expectations and that performance continuously improves.

Encouraging ownership and responsibility

While leaders set expectations, team members must ultimately take ownership of their work. When individuals feel personally responsible for outcomes, accountability becomes intrinsic rather than imposed. Empowering individuals to take ownership creates a sense of pride and commitment to the work they do.

Empowering team members: Empowerment comes from trust and autonomy. Leaders should equip team members with the tools, resources, and decision-making power they need to succeed. For instance, if a project leader has a clear goal but limited autonomy, they may feel stifled. By granting appropriate authority, leaders empower team members to take initiative and ownership. Empowerment also means trusting individuals to make decisions and solve problems on their own, rather than micromanaging their every move. This trust encourages individuals to take ownership and deliver results.

Creating a culture of accountability: Accountability thrives in a culture where it is embraced, not feared. Leaders can foster this by modeling accountability themselves. When a leader admits, "I missed a deadline on this report, and here's how I'll improve," they show that accountability applies to everyone, regardless of title. Such transparency builds trust and encourages others to take responsibility for their actions. In a culture of accountability, individuals feel safe to own up to their mistakes and learn from them, rather than fearing punishment.

Inspiring pride in results: When individuals see the impact of their contributions, they take greater pride in their work. Leaders should celebrate successes and highlight how individual efforts contributed to organizational goals. For example, publicly acknowledging a team member whose diligence helped secure a major win reinforces the value of ownership. Recognition not only boosts morale but also reinforces the importance of individual contributions to the team's success.

Ownership and responsibility are cultivated when team members feel trusted, valued, and connected to their outcomes. Accountability becomes a shared mindset rather than a top-down directive. Leaders who inspire ownership empower their teams to take full responsibility for their actions and the results they produce.

Enforcing consequences

Accountability cannot exist without consequences. When expectations are not met, leaders must address the gap. Consequences—both positive and negative—reinforce the importance of standards and drive behavior. Consequences ensure that individuals understand the seriousness of their commitments and that failure to meet expectations will have tangible results.

The role of consequences: Consequences are not about punishment; they are about integrity. If someone consistently underperforms without consequences, it sends a mes-

sage that expectations are optional. Conversely, when someone exceeds expectations, rewards signal that their efforts
are valued. Leaders must ensure that consequences are fair,
consistent, and applied across the board. Everyone, regardless of role, should be held to the same standards.

Fair and consistent enforcement: Fairness is critical.
Leaders must ensure that consequences are applied consistently across the team, regardless of relationships or sta-
tus. Favoritism undermines trust and erodes accountability.
Leaders should establish clear policies for performance outcomes, whether that involves additional support, corrective
action, or formal recognition. When consequences are en-
forced consistently, everyone understands the standards they
must meet, and there is no ambiguity about what happens
when those standards are not met.

Positive consequences: Positive reinforcement is powerful. Leaders should celebrate achievements through bonus-
es, public praise, or professional opportunities. For example, if a team member delivers exceptional results, offering
a leadership opportunity for the next project serves as both
a reward and motivation. Positive consequences help reinforce desired behaviors and encourage team members to
strive for excellence.

Addressing negative outcomes: When expectations are
unmet, leaders must intervene promptly and constructively.
A missed target may warrant a performance improvement
plan, additional training, or revised strategies. If a pattern
of underperformance persists despite intervention, leaders
must consider further consequences, such as reassignment
or termination. Though difficult, such actions are sometimes
necessary to maintain organizational integrity and morale.

By consistently enforcing consequences, leaders ensure
that accountability is non-negotiable. Standards matter—

and everyone must honor them. Leaders who uphold high standards create an environment where excellence is the expectation, not the exception.

Balancing tough love with support

Accountability without support is harsh; support without accountability is enabling. True leadership strikes a balance between the two. The most effective leaders know how to provide the right mix of tough love and support to help their teams succeed.

Offering resources and assistance: Holding team members to high standards does not mean leaving them to struggle. Leaders must ensure that individuals have the tools, knowledge, and support they need to meet expectations. For instance, if a team member struggles with a task, offering training or mentorship demonstrates a commitment to their success. Providing resources ensures that individuals have the ability to perform to the best of their abilities.

Providing encouragement during challenges: Challenges are inevitable. During tough times, leaders must provide encouragement while holding firm on expectations. For example, if a team faces setbacks on a project, a leader might say, "I know this is tough, but I believe in your ability to overcome these obstacles. What support do you need to get us back on track?" Providing encouragement helps individuals feel supported during difficult moments, while maintaining clear expectations keeps them focused on the goal.

Recognizing achievements and improvements: Recognition is the fuel that drives performance. Leaders should acknowledge not only big wins but also progress and effort. For instance, if a team member improves their performance after constructive feedback, recognizing that effort reinforces positive behavior. When individuals see that their hard work is noticed, they are more likely to continue striving for excellence.

Balancing accountability with compassion: Tough love requires compassion. A leader might need to say, "I care about your growth, and that's why I'm holding you to this standard. I know you can do better, and I'm here to help you get there." This balance ensures that accountability is seen as an investment in success, not as punishment. By offering both support and accountability, leaders create an environment where individuals feel valued and challenged simultaneously.

Tough love, when balanced with genuine support, fosters loyalty, resilience, and growth. It shows that leaders care about their team's success as much as their own.

Conclusion

Accountability is not about control—it's about creating an environment where individuals can grow and organizations can thrive. By establishing clear expectations, implementing measurable accountability systems, encouraging ownership, and enforcing fair consequences, leaders foster a culture of excellence and integrity.

Tough love, when executed with balance and compassion, transforms individuals and teams. It challenges people to rise to their potential while ensuring they have the support to succeed. The combination of high expectations and unwavering support creates a powerful dynamic: one where accountability becomes a shared value and success becomes a collective achievement.

In leadership, holding people's feet to the fire isn't about causing discomfort—it's about igniting their potential. Accountability, delivered with fairness and care, is one of the greatest gifts a leader can give. Through this approach, individuals grow, teams excel, and organizations achieve their vision.

7

TELL ME MORE, TELL ME MORE
– CULTIVATING A CULTURE OF FEEDBACK AND AUTHENTIC COMMUNICATION

recently attended our high school's performance of *Grease the Musical*. It was absolutely incredible! The energy, the singing, the dancing—everything was on point. I swayed, sang my heart out, and savored every moment. It was one of those experiences that leaves you feeling alive, connected, and grateful. At the end of the performance, the theatre director stood before the audience and thanked all of the students who made the production possible. She made sure to recognize every single role—from the curtain director to the stars of the play to the lighting crew, each contribution was celebrated. I looked on proudly as she named every person involved. Each individual had a part to play in bringing the performance to life.

As she spoke, I recalled each of their contributions. Without the meticulous attention of the lighting crew, for example, we would've missed key and special moments in the play. The way the lights shifted, accentuating the mood, guiding our attention, and creating moments of drama and emotion—it was all an integral part of the performance. Similarly, without feedback, we miss opportunities to be our best selves, celebrate our strengths, and improve our weaknesses. Feedback, like those spotlights, illuminates areas where we are getting things right and areas where we need to improve. It shows us both the beauty and the areas that need polishing, guiding us toward greater success.

Feedback is a tool for illumination, clarity, and progress. When used well, it helps individuals and organizations see things they otherwise might miss—whether it's strengths to build upon or weaknesses to address. However, its effectiveness often depends on the environment in which it is shared. In many organizations, power dynamics, fear of judgment, or a lack of trust can stifle the flow of authentic feedback. This prevents the full potential of feedback from being realized. Leaders must recognize the transformative power of feedback and work intentionally to create a culture where it can thrive. When approached with openness, curiosity, and courage, feedback becomes a catalyst for personal and organizational excellence, leading to continuous growth.

Leaders, especially CEOs, often find themselves isolated at the top, unable to access the authentic, unfiltered input they need to refine their leadership and drive their organizations forward. This isolation can create a disconnect between the leadership team and the rest of the organization, making it difficult for the organization to evolve in alignment with its vision. Creating a feedback-rich culture requires intentionality, humility, and courage. Feedback must flow freely across all levels, becoming the norm rather than an exception. This chapter explores how leaders can cultivate an environment where feedback is seen as a gift—one that fosters growth, innovation, and trust. By breaking down barriers, modeling openness, and acting on input, CEOs can inspire their teams to share honestly, creating a foundation for personal and organizational excellence.

Setting the stage for open communication

At its core, feedback is about trust and communication. Effective feedback is only possible when people feel safe enough to express their thoughts honestly. Before team members feel comfortable sharing their insights, leaders must establish the conditions necessary for open and honest dialogue. This is where the foundation for great feedback begins. It's about creating a culture where feedback is valued, encouraged, and normalized, rather than feared or avoided.

The importance of open communication

Open communication is a critical driver of continuous improvement. When team members can speak freely, organizations benefit from diverse perspectives, quicker problem-solving, and stronger relationships. But too often, communication is stifled by an unspoken fear: *Will my honesty cost me my job?* In organizations where communication is restricted by hierarchical barriers or the fear of backlash, innovation and progress are hampered. Leaders must proactively address this fear and set a tone where feedback is not only welcomed but valued. This starts with creating a safe environment where honesty is seen as an asset, not a threat.

Leaders must recognize that they hold the responsibility for setting this tone. By establishing clear expectations that communication should be open, candid, and solution-focused, leaders can create a space where everyone feels their voice matters. Feedback is a tool for growth, and when team members understand that their input is encouraged and appreciated, they will be more likely to contribute.

Fostering psychological safety

To encourage open communication, leaders must prioritize psychological safety—an environment where team members feel safe taking risks, voicing opinions, and sharing concerns without fear of punishment or embarrassment. Psychological safety isn't about eliminating conflict or disagreement; it's about fostering a space where disagreement and feedback can be handled constructively. In fact, constructive conflict is often essential for growth and innovation, and leaders should be proactive in normalizing it.

Leaders can establish psychological safety by:

- **Actively inviting input:** By regularly saying things like, "I value your perspective—what do you think?" leaders can create opportunities for dialogue. These simple words signal that everyone's opinion matters, which encourages people to speak up.

- **Demonstrating empathy:** Actively listening and acknowledging the challenges or emotions that team members experience helps to build trust. When leaders show empathy, they let team members know they are seen and heard, which fosters open communication.

- **Responding non-defensively:** When leaders receive feedback, it's vital to handle it with calmness and curiosity. Leaders who respond defensively push feedback underground and discourage future dialogue. Instead, they should view feedback as an opportunity to learn and grow. Leaders who model receptivity help to establish a culture where feedback is an ongoing, constructive exchange.

Leading by example

Leaders must walk the talk. By being open to feedback, showing vulnerability, and demonstrating a growth mindset, they set a powerful precedent for others to follow. For example, a CEO who admits, "I made a mistake here, and I'd appreciate your thoughts on how we can avoid this next time," shows humility and encourages others to speak up. This transparency models that leaders, too, are learning and evolving. It shows that they view feedback not as a threat but as a valuable tool for improvement. When leadership embraces feedback, it creates a trickle-down effect, encouraging the entire team to do the same.

Leadership sets the tone for the organization. If leaders embrace feedback, the team will follow suit. The example set by leadership, in both behavior and attitude, shapes the organization's feedback culture. A leader who is receptive, open, and willing to act on feedback establishes trust and sets the expectation that feedback is an essential part of the organization's culture.

Creating structured feedback mechanisms

While openness and trust are foundational to effective feedback, it's important to remember that effective feedback also requires structure. Without formal systems, feedback risks being inconsistent or ineffective. The absence of structure can leave people unsure of when, where, or how to share feedback, which reduces its impact.

Implementing regular feedback sessions

Regular feedback sessions, such as monthly check-ins, quarterly reviews, or anonymous surveys, create dedicated spaces for input. These sessions give team members a chance to prepare their thoughts and feel confident in sharing them. Setting regular, predictable feedback touchpoints signals to the team that feedback is valued and will be acted upon. These structured sessions reduce the anxiety or fear that often accompanies informal or impromptu feedback exchanges.

For example:

- **1:1 meetings**: Providing a private space for team members to share concerns and suggestions directly with their leaders. This is particularly important for issues that may feel too sensitive to bring up in larger meetings.

- **360-degree feedback**: Gathering insights from peers, managers, and direct reports to create a holistic view of performance. This method reduces bias and encourages a fuller understanding of how one's leadership is perceived at different levels.

- **Perception surveys**: Encouraging candid feedback through surveys can help strengthen the courage organizations need and eliminate the fear of retaliation.

However, anonymous surveys often undermine this courage. While I'm not a fan of anonymous surveys, I do support perception surveys in general, as they are an efficient way to gather both qualitative and quantitative feedback, while still encouraging openness and honesty.

Constructive feedback frameworks

Feedback needs to be clear, actionable, and constructive. Leaders can introduce frameworks like the **SBI (Situation-Behavior-Impact)** model, which focuses on specific examples to reduce ambiguity. This model ensures that feedback is actionable by linking behaviors to concrete outcomes. For instance:

- "In yesterday's meeting (Situation), when you dismissed the team's concerns quickly (Behavior), it made them feel undervalued (Impact)."

By providing training on such frameworks, leaders ensure that everyone in the organization can deliver feedback effectively and with care. These structured models make feedback less personal and more about behavior and results, which increases its effectiveness.

Equipping teams with feedback skills

Not everyone is naturally comfortable giving or receiving feedback. To create a feedback-rich culture, leaders must provide training sessions or workshops that build these skills. Emphasizing active listening, empathy, and clarity ensures that feedback is productive rather than harmful. These sessions can teach team members how to provide both positive and constructive feedback, which improves communication and strengthens relationships within teams.

Overcoming power dynamics

One of the greatest obstacles to honest feedback is the presence of power differentials. It can be intimidating for team members to provide candid input to someone who controls their job or career. When employees feel they might suffer professional consequences for speaking up, they will likely hold back, missing the opportunity to provide critical insights. Leaders must actively dismantle these barriers to create a level playing field where feedback can flow freely, regardless of title or position.

Recognizing the impact of power

Power, whether real or perceived, shapes how feedback flows within an organization. When employees feel that their feedback might be ignored or met with retaliation, they are less likely to speak up. CEOs must acknowledge these challenges and openly communicate their desire for open, unfiltered feedback. For example:

- "I know it can feel uncomfortable to provide feedback to me as your leader, but I truly value your perspective. I want us to get better together, and your input is essential in helping me do that."

Acknowledging the challenge openly removes the stigma surrounding power dynamics and creates a safe space for honest communication. Leaders who show self-awareness and actively seek input from all levels are better able to foster a culture of openness.

Fostering mutual trust and respect

Leaders can break down power dynamics by emphasizing shared goals and creating an atmosphere of mutual respect. When feedback exchanges feel collaborative rather than evaluative, employees are more likely to be candid. For example, using phrases like "Help me understand …" or "What would you do differently if you were in my position?" invites team members to contribute as equals. This approach makes feedback less about authority and more about collaboration and continuous improvement.

Encouraging candid conversations

To overcome hesitation, leaders should actively ask for feedback on specific areas. Broad questions like, "Do you have feedback for me?" can feel intimidating and vague. By being specific, leaders reduce the perceived risk of sharing feedback. Examples include:

- "How could I have handled that presentation better?"

- "Is there anything I'm doing that's making your work harder?"

Being specific about the areas where feedback is desired makes it easier for team members to provide practical, actionable input. It also signals that the leader genuinely wants to improve and values their team's perspective.

Acting on feedback and driving change

Soliciting feedback is only half the battle—acting on it is what transforms organizations and builds trust. Without follow-through, feedback loses its power, and team members become disillusioned. Feedback without action erodes credibility and discourages future honesty. Leaders must demonstrate a genuine commitment to change in order to inspire continued openness.

Demonstrating commitment to action

When leaders receive feedback, they must demonstrate a commitment to driving change. This involves:

- **Acknowledging the feedback openly**: "I heard your concerns about communication delays, and I'm committed to improving." Acknowledging the feedback shows that it has been received and valued.

- **Creating an action plan**: Clearly outlining the steps for addressing the feedback and assigning ownership ensures that the feedback leads to tangible change.

- **Following up**: Regularly updating the team on progress and outcomes shows that feedback results in measurable improvements. This reinforces the value of feedback and strengthens trust.

Encouraging accountability

Leaders must hold themselves and their teams accountable for acting on feedback. Setting clear timelines and responsibilities ensures that feedback doesn't get lost in the shuffle. For example:

- "You suggested a new process for onboarding—let's implement it next month and evaluate its impact in three months."

By ensuring that feedback is acted upon, leaders demonstrate their commitment to continuous improvement and accountability.

Celebrating successes

Leaders should celebrate wins that stem from feedback. When positive outcomes occur—whether it's improved team performance, smoother processes, or increased trust—these successes should be publicly recognized. Celebrating these results reinforces the value of feedback and encourages a culture of ongoing reflection and improvement. Publicly recognizing contributions also encourages continued openness and fosters a positive, feedback-friendly environment.

Nurturing a supportive feedback ecosystem

Feedback thrives when it is embedded into the organization's culture as an ongoing, continuous process rather than a one-time event. A true feedback ecosystem is one where feedback is normalized and woven into everyday interactions.

Building feedback mechanisms

Leaders can establish regular feedback rituals to normalize open communication. Examples include:

- **"Feedback Fridays"**: A dedicated time each week for team members to share reflections and suggestions. This simple, consistent ritual fosters an ongoing conversation about improvement.

- **After-action reviews**: Holding a debrief after projects to discuss what went well and what can be improved. This allows teams to learn from each experience and continually enhance their performance.

- **Check-in surveys**: Short, frequent surveys that monitor team morale and gather quick input. These allow leaders to stay in tune with their team's needs and concerns.

Establishing feedback loops

Feedback should flow in all directions—top-down, bottom-up, and peer-to-peer. Creating structured feedback loops ensures ongoing dialogue and continuous improvement. For instance, a CEO might share feedback received with their leadership team and outline the plan to act on it. This transparency reinforces the idea that feedback is not just for evaluation, but for positive change.

Sustaining a culture of feedback

Feedback must be woven into the organization's DNA. Leaders can foster this culture by:

- **Encouraging reflection**: Asking team members to reflect on their performance and solicit feedback from peers.

- **Modeling ongoing growth**: Leaders should regularly share what they're learning from feedback, showing that growth is a continuous journey for everyone.

- **Providing tools and resources**: Equip teams with platforms, workshops, and processes that make giving and receiving feedback easier.

When feedback becomes a habit, it ceases to feel like a critique and instead becomes a normal, valued part of organizational life. It becomes embedded into the organization's daily rhythm, a natural part of how things get done.

Conclusion

Feedback, while not always comfortable, is not a burden; it is a gift. Leaders who actively seek and embrace feedback demonstrate humility, trust, and a commitment to growth. By fostering an environment of psychological safety, dismantling power dynamics, and acting on input, CEOs can create a culture where honest communication thrives.

A feedback-rich culture is not built overnight. It requires courage, consistency, and a willingness to embrace vulnerability. Yet, the rewards are profound: stronger relationships, improved performance, and an organization that continuously learns and grows.

As leaders, the choice is clear: Will we seek feedback and unlock the potential of our teams, or will we let power, fear, and ego keep us in the dark? By cultivating a culture of feedback, we not only elevate ourselves but empower those around us to contribute to a shared vision of success. Feedback is not just a conversation—it's a catalyst for excellence.

8

STICKS IN A BUNDLE
– FOSTERING GENUINE TEAM CONNECTION

There is a powerful African proverb that states, "Sticks in a bundle are unbreakable." It's a simple yet profound truth: While a single stick can be easily snapped, a tightly bound bundle of sticks is resilient and strong. The same principle applies to leadership teams. A CEO's success—and by extension, the success of the entire organization—depends not just on individual brilliance but on the strength of a unified, collaborative leadership team.

This idea is not just a metaphor; it's a fundamental truth that can shape the way leaders build their teams. A CEO can have all the right strategies, skills, and vision, but without the support, alignment, and collaboration of their leadership team, even the best ideas can falter. A leadership team that is fragmented, disjointed, or disconnected will struggle to achieve collective goals and create lasting impact. On the other hand, a cohesive leadership team, one that works together with trust, respect, and shared vision, becomes a force capable of achieving extraordinary results.

A CEO's role goes far beyond performance reviews or strategic planning. It extends into the realm of culture-building, fostering an environment where leaders trust each other, work collaboratively, and see themselves as part of something larger than their individual roles. When executive teams are unified and cohesive, their collective strength becomes a driving force for organizational excellence. In contrast, fragmentation among leaders erodes trust, silos innovation, and stifles progress. The strength of unity and collaboration within a leadership team cannot be overstated. When CEOs intentionally invest in this unity, they lay the foundation for success that transcends individual contributions, creating a team that is greater than the sum of its parts.

This chapter explores the importance of unity within leadership teams, offering strategies for cultivating trust, enhancing team dynamics, and promoting authentic communication. By nurturing relationships, celebrating shared experiences, and fostering a sense of belonging, CEOs can unlock the full potential of their teams, building a resilient and energetic leadership culture that propels the organization forward. The process is not an overnight one, but it is one of the most rewarding investments a CEO can make in the success and sustainability of their organization.

The power of team synergy

A strong leadership team is not just a collection of talented individuals; it is a synergistic force that multiplies the impact of each member's contributions. Synergy occurs when diverse perspectives, skills, and experiences come together, generating innovative solutions that no single individual could achieve alone. Synergy enables teams to leverage their differences as strengths, resulting in more creative solutions, faster problem-solving, and the ability to overcome obstacles more efficiently.

The importance of teamwork in driving success

Teamwork is the backbone of organizational success. A cohesive leadership team sets the tone for collaboration throughout the company. When executives work together toward shared goals, they model the behavior expected of others. Their unity fosters alignment, accelerates decision-making, and enhances operational efficiency. A leadership team that collaborates effectively can streamline processes, reduce redundancy, and create a culture where working together is second nature.

The dynamics of a strong leadership team are reflected in the larger organization. Employees observe how their leaders interact, how decisions are made, and how challenges are addressed. A cohesive team, where collaboration is prioritized, sends a powerful message to the rest of the organization about the value of teamwork and collaboration. Leaders who model unity inspire their teams to work together, share knowledge, and build stronger, more effective relationships across departments.

Diverse perspectives drive innovation

Diversity within a leadership team—whether in backgrounds, skill sets, or perspectives—is an untapped resource for creativity. CEOs who embrace this diversity reap the rewards of more comprehensive problem-solving. For instance, while one leader may bring analytical rigor, another may excel in creative strategy, and yet another in operational execution. When these strengths are combined, the team develops holistic solutions that benefit the entire organization. Diversity brings different ideas, approaches, and solutions to the table, creating an environment where innovation can thrive.

By building teams with diverse backgrounds and experiences, CEOs create a rich environment for new ideas to emerge. For example, a team that includes both tech-savvy leaders and those with a deep understanding of the customer experience can develop products and services that resonate on both a functional and emotional level. The beauty of a diverse team lies in its ability to approach problems from different angles and find solutions that no one individual could have envisioned.

Case study: the power of collaboration

Consider a global technology firm that faced declining market share. The CEO brought the leadership team together for intensive collaboration. By combining marketing insights, engineering solutions, and financial strategies, the team identified a market gap and pivoted to launch a groundbreaking product. This success was not the result of one department's brilliance but rather the leadership team's collective effort. It was a true example of synergy—where each leader's unique perspective and expertise contributed to a unified solution that propelled the company forward.

This case underscores a critical truth: No matter how talented an individual leader may be, their success is often tied to the collective strength of the team around them. When leaders unite their strengths, they create outcomes far greater than the sum of their individual efforts. Collaboration and synergy are not just buzzwords—they are the foundation of transformative leadership.

Building trust and connection

Trust is the cornerstone of any successful team. Without it, collaboration breaks down, and even the most talented teams fall short. For a CEO, building trust within the leadership team is both a responsibility and a strategic priority. Trust enables leaders to have candid conversations, resolve conflicts effectively, and make decisions in alignment with the organization's vision. It also promotes the vulnerability needed for innovation, where team members can freely share ideas, admit mistakes, and learn from one another.

The role of trust in collaboration

Trust creates an environment where team members feel safe to share ideas, admit mistakes, and take risks. It eliminates the fear of judgment and fosters vulnerability, which is essential for innovation and problem-solving. Leaders who trust one another can navigate conflict constructively and align on difficult decisions without questioning each other's motives. This is huge. In such an environment, ideas are exchanged freely, and the focus shifts from protecting individual egos to finding the best solutions for the organization.

Trust also accelerates decision-making. When trust is high, leaders don't waste time second-guessing one another or worrying about hidden agendas. Instead, they move quickly, confident that their peers have the organization's best interests at heart. This efficiency is critical in fast-paced environments where the ability to act decisively can make the difference between success and failure.

Strategies for enhancing trust

1. **Transparency**: CEOs should model transparency by sharing information openly and inviting team members to do the same. When people feel informed, they are more likely to trust leadership and each other. Transparency fosters a sense of fairness and equity, ensuring that everyone is on the same page and working toward the same goals. This clarity is essential for aligning the leadership team and ensuring that decisions are made with the best possible information.

2. **Active listening**: Demonstrating genuine curiosity and attentiveness when others speak builds mutual respect. When leaders feel heard, trust deepens. Active listening signals to team members that their opinions and ideas are valued, which strengthens relationships and creates an environment where open dialogue is encouraged.

3. **Consistency**: Leaders must show up consistently—in words, actions, and commitments. Following through on promises strengthens credibility and builds trust over time. Consistency is a powerful tool for creating stability within a leadership team. When leaders consistently honor their commitments, they establish a foundation of reliability that allows trust to flourish.

Team-building activities to foster connection

Trust isn't built overnight, but it can be nurtured through intentional activities. CEOs can facilitate team-building exercises that help leaders connect on a personal level and foster deeper relationships.

- **Team retreats**: Taking leaders out of their day-to-day environment allows them to connect on a deeper level. Activities like group problem-solving challenges or informal dinners promote bonding and create opportunities for team members to relate to one another outside of the office. Retreats also allow leaders to step back from the daily grind and reflect on their collective mission and goals.

- **Vulnerability exercises**: Encouraging leaders to share their personal stories, challenges, or values fosters understanding and empathy. When leaders are vulnerable with one another, they build trust by showing that they are human and not just authority figures. These exercises promote connection by reminding team members that they share common experiences and emotions.

- **Trust-building workshops**: Facilitating structured conversations around strengths, challenges, and collaboration styles helps team members appreciate each other's contributions. These workshops provide a safe space for leaders to discuss their working styles and learn how to better support one another. The more team members understand each other, the stronger the foundation of trust becomes.

When trust flourishes, leaders become allies—united by shared purpose and mutual respect. This unity enables them to tackle challenges together, make better decisions, and guide the organization toward long-term success.

Enhancing team dynamics

In today's fast-paced and often hybrid work environments, fostering meaningful team interactions can be challenging. Yet, strong team dynamics are essential for maintaining cohesion and alignment. The ability of a leadership team to work well together, despite geographical barriers or differing schedules, directly impacts the organization's overall performance. Leaders who invest in their team dynamics create a culture of collaboration, where individuals feel supported and empowered to contribute their best work.

The hybrid work challenge

Hybrid and remote work have transformed the way leadership teams interact. While virtual tools enable connectivity, they can also create barriers to building deep, personal relationships. Leaders may feel isolated or disconnected from their peers, undermining the unity needed for high performance. In a virtual environment, team members might struggle to build the same level of rapport and trust that comes naturally in face-to-face interactions.

To overcome this challenge, CEOs must actively create spaces for connection—both virtually and in person. Without these intentional efforts, virtual teams can slip into transactional relationships that lack the depth needed for effective collaboration. Leaders must prioritize connection just as much as they prioritize operational outcomes, recognizing that the two are deeply intertwined.

Facilitating meaningful interactions

To counteract these challenges, CEOs must intentionally create opportunities for connection:

- **Regular check-ins**: Schedule consistent meetings that balance operational updates with time for personal connection. Start meetings with a "team check-in," where leaders share their current priorities, challenges, or successes. These informal moments build rapport and remind the team that they are working together toward a shared mission.

- **In-person experiences**: Plan regular off-site meetings or retreats where leaders can build rapport face-to-face. Activities that encourage collaboration, such as brainstorming sessions or strategy workshops, strengthen relationships and provide opportunities for spontaneous conversations and ideas to emerge. In-person interactions help solidify the bonds formed through virtual channels.

- **Virtual bonding moments**: Incorporate interactive exercises into virtual meetings, such as "quick wins" celebrations, virtual coffee chats, or storytelling rounds where leaders share professional or personal highlights. These activities create opportunities for leaders to connect on a personal level, reinforcing their sense of belonging and mutual support.

The power of shared experiences

Team retreats, collaborative projects, and shared challenges bring leadership teams closer together. Shared experiences build camaraderie and remind leaders that they are part of something larger. For example, an executive team that tackles a difficult project together often emerges stronger, bonded by their collective effort and resilience. The memories and experiences created during such projects become the glue that holds the team together, even in challenging times.

When team dynamics are intentionally nurtured, collaboration becomes natural, even in the most challenging circumstances. Leadership teams that invest in their relationships not only become more effective, but also create a culture where teamwork is valued and prioritized. These teams can weather any storm and continue to thrive, no matter the challenges they face.

Promoting authentic communication

Authentic communication is the lifeblood of any cohesive team. Without open dialogue, misunderstandings fester, and relationships weaken. Leaders must create an environment where honest, constructive communication is encouraged and valued. When leaders communicate openly and authentically, they not only improve decision-making but also foster a culture of trust and respect.

Creating safe spaces for vulnerability

Authentic communication begins with vulnerability. Leaders must feel safe sharing their perspectives, concerns, and mistakes. A CEO can model this by admitting their own challenges or asking for help: "I don't have all the answers—what do you think we should do?" This openness encourages others to communicate honestly without fear of judgment. When vulnerability is embraced at the top, it creates a ripple effect throughout the organization.

Leaders who practice vulnerability create a culture where it is safe for others to do the same. By modeling openness, CEOs set the tone for the rest of the organization, encouraging employees at all levels to communicate with authenticity and transparency.

Techniques for fostering authentic communication

1. **Storytelling**: Encouraging leaders to share personal or professional stories deepens understanding and connection. Stories provide context, humanize individuals, and create common ground. When leaders share their journeys, challenges, and successes, they not only build trust but also inspire others to do the same.

2. **Constructive feedback**: Introduce feedback frameworks like "What's going well, and what can we improve?" to facilitate honest yet supportive conversations. Constructive feedback helps team members grow while maintaining a sense of mutual respect. It creates a safe space for continuous learning and improvement.

3. **Personality assessments**: Tools like Myers–Briggs, DISC, or StrengthsFinder can help team members better understand their communication styles, preferences, and strengths. These assessments foster empathy and improve communication by highlighting the unique ways each leader approaches work and interacts with others.

The value of informal conversations

Not all meaningful communication happens in formal meetings. Informal conversations—over coffee, during team lunches, or in virtual "watercooler" chats—are essential for building trust and camaraderie. Leaders should create time and space for these moments to occur naturally. These informal interactions often lead to deeper insights and more authentic relationships than structured meetings alone.

When communication is authentic, leadership teams develop deeper connections, resolve conflicts faster, and align more effectively. Authenticity fosters a sense of belonging and trust, creating an environment where leaders can share openly and work together more effectively.

Sustaining team unity

Building team unity is not a one-time effort; it requires on-going attention and nurturing, especially during times of change or challenge. Unity can be fragile, and external pressures can test the strength of a leadership team. Whether facing market shifts, organizational restructuring, or leadership transitions, CEOs must prioritize team cohesion to keep their leadership team strong and focused on shared goals.

Maintaining cohesion through change

Change—whether organizational restructuring, leadership transitions, or market shifts—can test a team's unity. CEOs must keep the team grounded by reinforcing shared goals, acknowledging challenges, and celebrating progress. Consistent communication during change ensures that leaders remain aligned and focused on common objectives. It also provides reassurance that, despite external disruptions, the leadership team is united and committed to navigating change together.

Celebrating successes and acknowledging challenges

Recognition is a powerful tool for maintaining team morale and unity. Celebrating successes, both big and small, reminds leaders of their collective achievements. Equally important is acknowledging challenges openly. A CEO who says, "This was a tough quarter, but we showed resilience as a team," reinforces the value of shared effort.

Acknowledging challenges and celebrating progress ensures that the leadership team stays motivated, focused, and united during times of uncertainty. It reinforces the idea that, together, the team can overcome any obstacle and continue to drive the organization toward success.

A road map for continuous team development

- **Regular check-ins**: Keep the pulse on team dynamics through surveys, open forums, or 1:1 conversations.

- **Annual team retreats**: Provide opportunities for reflection, bonding, and strategic alignment.

- **Ongoing development**: Invest in leadership training and team-building initiatives to strengthen collaboration over time.

The CEO's role is to continuously foster an environment where unity thrives, ensuring the team remains strong, resilient, and focused on shared goals.

Conclusion

A unified leadership team is not only resilient but also transformative. By fostering trust, promoting authentic communication, and cultivating shared experiences, CEOs can build a leadership culture rooted in collaboration, belonging, and mutual support.

Team cohesion is not a luxury—it is a necessity for sustainable success. When leaders see themselves as part of a greater whole, their collective strength propels the organization forward, driving innovation, resilience, and a shared commitment to achieving extraordinary results. By prioritizing relationships, fostering trust, and embracing the power of unity, CEOs can unlock the full potential of their leadership teams and ensure that their organizations are un-breakable—just like sticks in a bundle.

The reality is, in many of our organizations, we work to-gether nine to twelve hours a day or more. We deserve joy. We deserve environments that don't inflame our nervous systems. We deserve teammates we actually enjoy doing hard work alongside. When CEOs intentionally cultivate team cohesion, they don't just build stronger organizations; they create spaces where people feel seen, valued, and con-nected—where working together becomes a sustainable source of energy, fulfillment, and collective pride.

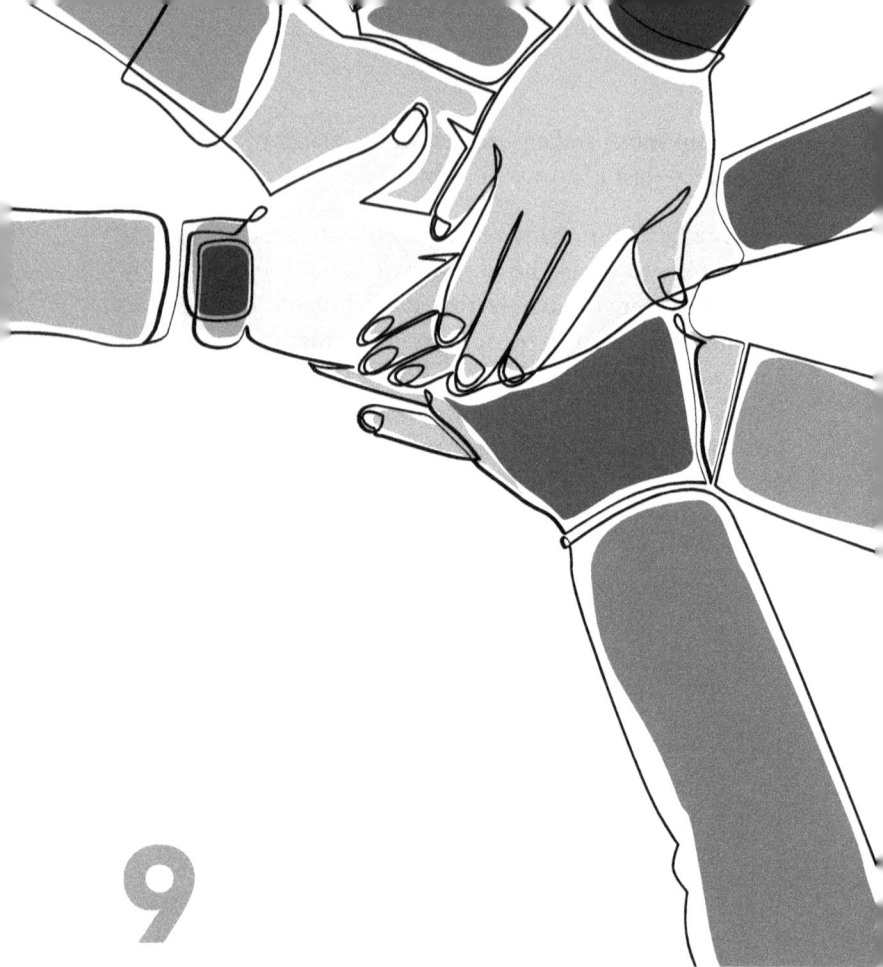

9

REST
– THE
MARATHON AS
A STRATEGIC
IMPERATIVE

When I began my journey as a leader, I carried an ambitious goal: I would "fix" the executive leadership team by December of my first year. It seemed like a reasonable and even noble aspiration at the time—after all, Rome wasn't built in a day, but surely a year would suffice to achieve alignment, cohesion, and peak performance among our leaders. I was determined to address team dynamics, improve communication, and ensure that we would operate like a finely tuned machine. The reality, however, was different than I expected. It took three long years to build the foundation for a truly cohesive team, and even now, as the years have passed, we are still working on it. New team members come aboard, relationships evolve, and the dynamics shift, constantly challenging our leadership cohesion and team energy.

This experience, while humbling, taught me a profound lesson: Leadership development is not a sprint but a marathon. In the high-stakes and fast-moving world of organizational leadership, the journey toward sustained success demands much more than technical expertise, endless energy, or short bursts of effort. It requires emotional investment, strategic pacing, and, perhaps most importantly, periods of rest and renewal. I had initially believed that continuous progress, without pause, was the key to achieving rapid success. But over time, I realized that constant movement doesn't always equate to progress. The most successful teams take time to rest, recover, and reflect, and this rest is not a weakness but an essential part of the work itself.

The notion of rest is often undervalued in high-performing organizations. I have been guilty of this mindset. Too often, leaders equate progress with continuous motion, assuming that taking breaks will slow momentum or signal weakness to the rest of the organization. Yet, like any long-distance athlete knows, rest is not a break from the work—it is part of the work. Without it, even the strongest teams will eventually falter under the weight of burnout, diminished creativity, and fractured relationships. Rest ensures that teams continue to perform at their best, that their creativity remains sharp, and that they stay connected in ways that foster collaboration and innovation.

This chapter explores why rest is not just a luxury or a sign of indulgence but rather a strategic imperative for leadership teams. It examines the true cost of relentless output, the importance of recognizing energy depletion, and the value of structured pauses to sustain long-term success. By shifting from a sprint mindset to a marathon mentality, CEOs can create environments that foster resilience, innovation, and longevity within their leadership teams. These teams will not only endure but thrive, achieving extraordinary results with stamina and vitality.

The significance of sustainable energy

In the relentless pursuit of excellence, leadership teams often operate at an unsustainable pace. There is an internal drive, fueled by the desire to achieve more, faster, and better. Yet, high performance demands not just commitment, creativity, and resilience, but an understanding that these are finite resources. To achieve sustained success, leaders must learn how to balance output with periodic renewal.

The cost of continuous output

Constant motion without rest inevitably leads to diminishing returns. In the business world, this manifests as a perpetual cycle of meetings, decision-making, and high-stakes problem-solving. While this effort might yield short-term results, over time, the toll on energy, creativity, and emotional well-being becomes evident. Studies have shown that chronic overwork results in:

- **Increased stress levels, leading to burnout:** When individuals are consistently pushed beyond their limits without time for recovery, stress mounts, making it harder to concentrate, make decisions, and maintain mental clarity.

- **Decreased productivity and focus due to fatigue:** The human brain, much like any other resource, can only be pushed so far before it becomes less effective. Fatigue dulls focus, causes mistakes, and hinders a team's ability to think critically.

- **Declines in creativity and problem-solving capacity:** The ability to think innovatively is directly impacted by a lack of rest. The mental energy required for creativity diminishes when the mind is exhausted.

When exhaustion sets in, a leadership team's performance plateaus. Morale drops, productivity declines, and creativity stalls. Teams operating in perpetual sprint mode may achieve short-term wins, but they risk long-term breakdowns in energy, cohesion, and strategic progress.

The impact of team energy on performance

Leadership teams are ecosystems—what affects one person's energy level will, inevitably, affect the whole group. High-functioning teams thrive on shared energy, collaboration, and alignment. When one team member experiences fatigue, it ripples throughout the organization. If left unchecked, this ripple effect can disrupt relationships, hinder communication, and erode trust. As energy wanes, these core components of high-performing teams are jeopardized.

Sustainable leadership starts at the top. CEOs and senior leaders must model the behaviors they want to see in their teams. Leaders who prioritize their own rest, well-being, and reflection set a powerful example. Their actions signal to their teams that well-being is an essential part of sustained performance, not an afterthought. When leaders take time for themselves, they are better equipped to care for and support their teams, fostering a healthy, energized, and resilient culture.

Recognizing energy depletion

The first step in managing team energy is recognizing when it's running low. Awareness is key—leaders must develop an acute sensitivity to the signs of fatigue, not just in individual team members, but also in the overall dynamic of the group.

Signs of team fatigue

Burnout rarely happens overnight. It builds gradually, often unnoticed, until its impact becomes severe. For leaders, it is crucial to recognize early warning signs of fatigue to address the issue before it leads to deeper problems. Some key indicators of team fatigue include:

1. **Decreased motivation:** A noticeable drop in enthusiasm, engagement, or willingness to take initiative often signals that the team is burning out. Tasks that once energized the team now feel like burdens.

2. **Heightened stress levels:** Increased tension, irritability, and conflict within the team are red flags. Disagreements may become more frequent, and cooperation becomes strained.

3. **Declines in productivity:** When tasks take longer, mistakes increase, and the creativity that once fueled innovation begins to dwindle, it's clear that fatigue is taking its toll.

4. **Emotional withdrawal:** Team members may disengage emotionally, avoid collaboration, or demonstrate apathy

toward outcomes. This emotional distancing is often a defense mechanism against burnout.

Individual vs. collective depletion

While fatigue may begin at an individual level, its ripple effects are felt by the entire team. A burned-out leader can significantly lower the morale of others, much like a single sick tree in a forest that affects the health of the surrounding trees. In a leadership team, if one person is disengaged or overwhelmed, it's easy for the negative energy to spread. CEOs must pay attention not only to individual well-being but also to the collective energy of the group to identify when intervention is needed.

Communication and feedback

Creating open channels for honest communication is essential in maintaining awareness of team energy levels. Leaders must foster a culture where team members feel safe sharing when they are feeling overwhelmed, stressed, or need additional support. CEOs can encourage dialogue through:

- **Regular 1:1 check-ins:** These sessions allow leaders to assess individual well-being and ensure that no one is silently struggling.

- **Well-being surveys:** These can be helpful for gathering insights on team energy levels, workload, and any stressors that may be impacting performance.

- **Team discussions:** Normalizing conversations about stress and fatigue within the team helps reduce stigma and encourages collective responsibility for well-being.

By recognizing energy depletion early, leaders can step in before burnout takes hold, preserving both the vitality of the team and its momentum. This proactive approach is critical to maintaining high performance and team cohesion over the long haul.

Strategically navigating rest and reflection

Rest is not simply a passive activity; it is a strategic choice. When approached with intention, rest fuels resilience, creativity, and long-term progress. The key lies in embedding practices that allow both individuals and teams to pause, reflect, and renew on a regular basis.

Building resilience

Resilience is the ability to navigate challenges and bounce back stronger. It is not built through constant output but through balanced cycles of effort and recovery. CEOs can foster resilience within their teams by encouraging practices that help leaders and team members recharge and refocus. These might include:

- **Mindfulness practices:** Activities like meditation, journaling, or quiet reflection can help leaders manage stress and enhance focus.

- **Recovery rituals:** Whether through physical exercise, engaging in hobbies, or spending quality time with family, encouraging leaders to step away from work to recharge is vital for long-term energy renewal.

Structured rest periods

Scheduled breaks—whether daily, quarterly, or annually—are essential for maintaining team energy. CEOs can incorporate structured rest into the work cycle to ensure that the team remains energized and engaged. Some ideas for implementing structured rest include:

- **Breaks between high-intensity projects:** Avoid scheduling back-to-back major initiatives without adequate recovery time in between.

- **Leadership retreats:** Organize off-site gatherings that provide the team with an opportunity to reflect, regroup, and realign their goals, away from the pressures of daily operations.

- **Sabbaticals:** Encourage leaders to take extended breaks when needed. These periods of extended rest allow individuals to recharge and gain fresh perspectives, ultimately benefiting the team when they return.

Structured rest allows teams to step back from the relentless pace of their work, evaluate their progress, and return with renewed focus, creativity, and energy.

Fostering a culture of self-care

- Sustainable leadership begins with a commitment to self-care. CEOs must emphasize the importance of mental, emotional, and physical well-being within their organizations. This can be achieved by:

- **Leading by example:** Prioritize your own health and rest as a visible commitment to balance. When leaders model healthy behaviors, it signals to the team that well-being is a priority.

- **Providing resources:** Offer wellness programs, leadership coaching, or flexible work schedules to support employee well-being.

- **Normalizing self-care:** Encourage leaders to take time off without guilt or fear of judgment. This removes the stigma around rest and promotes a culture of sustainability.

Rest is not indulgence; it is a deliberate strategy for maintaining excellence over the long term. Leaders who embrace self-care as a fundamental part of their role create environments that value energy, well-being, and balanced productivity.

Long-term vision and sustainability

Leadership is a marathon, not a sprint. Sustainable success requires careful pacing, endurance, and a deep commitment to long-term goals. It is not about sprinting toward an immediate goal at the expense of long-term health; it is about steady, intentional progress toward meaningful outcomes.

The marathon mentality

- Sprint cultures tend to prioritize quick wins at the expense of team health, long-term planning, and strategic reflection. In contrast, a marathon mindset emphasizes steady, significant but sometimes incremental progress. Leaders must recognize that achieving lasting organizational transformation takes time, patience, and sustained effort. For example:

- Building a cohesive leadership team may take years, not just a few months.

- Cultural change requires consistency, not quick fixes or temporary initiatives.

- Strategic goals should be approached with an incremental mindset, ensuring that adjustments and reflections are embedded in the process.

By pacing themselves and their teams, CEOs create an environment that promotes longevity, resilience, and continuous growth.

Balancing action and contemplation

Pauses are not moments of stagnation; they are opportunities for strategic reflection. When leadership teams step back from execution, they gain clarity, alignment, and perspective. Moments of contemplation allow leaders to:

- **Reassess priorities:** Ensure that the team's efforts remain aligned with the organization's long-term vision.

- **Identify challenges:** Spot gaps or blind spots that may have been overlooked during the hustle.

- **Reignite passion:** Reconnect with the organization's core purpose and goals, reigniting enthusiasm and commitment.

The value of stability and continuity

Longevity in leadership creates stability, consistency, and trust. High turnover within leadership teams disrupts progress and erodes cohesion. By prioritizing the well-being of their teams and fostering long-term growth, CEOs promote retention, ensuring leadership continuity that becomes a competitive advantage. A cohesive, long-standing leadership team provides the steady hand needed to navigate change and sustain growth.

Conclusion

The journey of leadership is not about speed; it is about building our organizations to last. Teams cannot thrive on relentless effort alone. To achieve extraordinary, long-term success, leaders must embrace rest as a strategic imperative—an essential component of their work, not an interruption of it.

Rest fuels resilience. Pauses spark creativity. Renewal fosters energy and innovation. By recognizing the signs of fatigue, fostering a culture of self-care, and strategically embedding rest into team dynamics, CEOs can nurture leadership teams that endure, adapt, and thrive.

When CEOs shift from a sprint mentality to a marathon mindset, they create leadership teams that are unbreakable, resilient, and prepared to achieve lasting success. Rest, reflection, and renewal are not luxuries; they are the foundations of sustainable greatness.

10

KEEP GOING – THE UNYIELDING PURSUIT OF A WINNING LEADERSHIP TEAM

When I gave birth to my first child, I had meticulously planned every detail. I read a myriad of books, attended multiple prenatal classes, and even crafted a vision in my mind of the "perfect" birth experience—one that would be calm, swift, and in complete control. I imagined a smooth and serene process, with minimal disruption. However, reality had other plans. Instead of a few hours of peaceful childbirth, I ended up in labor for an exhausting thirty-six hours. I cried tears of pain and frustration, suffered through moments of unimaginable discomfort, and at one point, I truly believed I wouldn't make it to the end. It was nothing like I had envisioned. But somehow, despite the overwhelming pain and the doubt that crept in at every corner, I made it through. I held on to hope, surrendered to the process, and persevered through those incredibly difficult moments. Today, as I look at my son, now a senior in high school preparing for college, I see that thirty-six-hour labor, taxing as it was, as one of the most meaningful and rewarding experiences of my life. It was a pivotal moment of transformation that I will forever cherish.

In much the same way, building and maintaining a winning leadership team is no different. It is a journey that demands patience, resilience, hard work, and sometimes even surrender. The process is not easy, and there will be moments of discomfort, frustration, and doubt along the way. There will be times when you feel as though you are not making any headway, and it may even seem like your team will never come together in the way you envisioned. But just as I learned through childbirth, some of the most remarkable outcomes in life are born out of the most arduous and challenging processes.

This chapter marks the culmination of the journey we have taken together throughout this book. Crafting a successful and cohesive leadership team is not something that happens overnight. It requires a relentless commitment to the vision, a willingness to push through difficulties, and a readiness to adapt and learn along the way. There will be setbacks, and there will be milestones, but the reward for those who stick with the process is extraordinary: teams that are aligned, unified, and capable of leading with strength, purpose, and a shared vision. These teams drive sustainable success and inspire others to follow.

As we close the final pages of this book, I invite you to reflect on the journey you have already begun or are about to embark on. Leadership is not a linear path, and it's not always easy, but it is always worth it. Let's explore the enduring power of perseverance, the joy found in celebrating progress, and the importance of maintaining a hopeful and determined outlook as you continue on this transformative journey.

Embracing persistence

Building a high-performing, cohesive leadership team requires a deep, unwavering commitment to the journey itself. Along the way, you will encounter moments of frustration, resistance, and even failure. But these obstacles are not signs of defeat—they are simply stepping stones, opportunities for growth and learning that will shape the team you are striving to create.

The role of perseverance in leadership development

Great leadership teams are not simply built with a stroke of luck or by chance. They are cultivated through intentional, consistent effort, trust-building, and the willingness to push through challenges, even when it feels impossible. Leadership development, much like personal growth, is a gradual process, with progress often unfolding at a slower pace than we expect. At times, it may even seem as though we're not making any significant progress. But each meeting, each difficult conversation, each leadership retreat is a step forward, even if the steps seem small. These moments contribute to the foundation of trust, alignment, and strength that will eventually make your team thrive.

A story of perseverance

I remember a time, early in my tenure as CEO, when the leadership team I both inherited and hired was struggling to connect. Communication was fractured, silos began to form, and morale across the team was plummeting. For a fleeting moment, I began to doubt whether true alignment would ever be possible for us. It felt like the weight of the challenges was too heavy to bear. But instead of abandoning the process altogether, I made the conscious decision to double down on our efforts. We dedicated ourselves to investing time and energy into team-building activities, established structures that encouraged honest feedback, and took the time to clearly define each individual's role and expectations within the team. These changes did not yield immediate results—there were still moments of tension, missed opportunities, and growing pains. But slowly, over time, trust began to grow. Today, when I reflect on that difficult period, I see it as a defining turning point in the life of our team—a testament to the power of perseverance and patience, and a clear example of how commitment can lead to breakthrough moments.

Practical strategies for staying resilient:

1. **Revisit your vision**: Whenever you find yourself feeling stuck or progress seems slow, take a step back and remind yourself and your team of the larger purpose. *Why are you doing this work? How does a strong leadership team impact the success of the organization?* Reconnecting with the big picture can help reignite passion and clarity.

2. **Break it down**: Set small, achievable milestones along the way. Each small success, no matter how seemingly insignificant, builds momentum and helps maintain motivation within the team.

3. **Adopt a growth mindset**: Shift your perspective on challenges and setbacks by viewing them as opportunities for learning and improvement. Instead of asking, "Why did this happen?" ask, "What can we learn from this experience, and how can we use it to become better moving forward?"

4. **Seek support**: Leadership can often feel lonely, and the weight of responsibility can be overwhelming at times. Reach out to mentors, trusted peers, or professional coaches for guidance, feedback, and perspective. They can provide invaluable support and help you maintain your sense of direction.

Persistence is the secret ingredient that leads to breakthroughs. Leaders who refuse to give up—despite setbacks, failures, and seemingly insurmountable obstacles—ultimately build teams that can achieve extraordinary things.

Celebrating progress

In the relentless pursuit of lofty goals, it's easy to overlook the progress you've made along the way. However, taking time to celebrate milestones, both big and small, is essential to sustaining energy, boosting morale, and keeping the momentum alive.

Reflecting on the journey

Building a leadership team is not just about the organization; it's about the individuals who make up that team. As trust deepens, communication strengthens, and alignment takes root, the leaders themselves grow into their full potential. It's essential to pause and reflect on this journey of growth, both at the team level and on a personal level.

Take a moment to ask yourself and your team:

- Where were we a year ago, and where are we now?

- What challenges have we overcome together, and what lessons have we learned along the way?

- What wins—big or small—can we celebrate, and how can we recognize our collective achievements?

By acknowledging progress, you not only affirm the hard work and dedication of your team members but also reinforce the value of the journey itself. This recognition builds momentum and keeps the energy flowing toward future goals.

Recognizing team achievements

Don't wait for the "big wins" to celebrate. Take time to honor every step forward. Whether it's completing a major project, achieving a strategic goal, or simply improving communication and trust within the team, every milestone deserves recognition. Here are a few practical ways to celebrate:

- **Publicly recognize contributions**: Take a moment in team meetings to recognize individual achievements and the collective effort of the team.

- **Host celebratory events**: Whether it's a dinner, a retreat, or a small gathering, taking time to reflect and celebrate is a meaningful way to recognize progress.

- **Share success stories**: Share stories of the team's successes across the broader organization. This not only boosts morale but also serves as an inspiration for others.

The power of gratitude

Gratitude is one of the most powerful motivators. A simple "thank you" can go a long way in making team members feel seen, valued, and appreciated. As a CEO, acknowledging the hard work, growth, and contributions of your team fosters loyalty, strengthens relationships, and cultivates a culture of respect and recognition.

Progress is always worth celebrating. When you take the time to honor your achievements, no matter how small, it reminds the team of how far they've come and reignites their commitment to the road ahead.

Looking ahead

While celebrating progress is vital, great leaders understand that the journey of leadership never truly ends. To sustain momentum, you must maintain a commitment to growth, continuous improvement, and a forward-focused vision.

The importance of continuous improvement

The most successful leadership teams are those that never settle. Once a goal is achieved, new aspirations must be set. A mindset of continuous improvement ensures that the team remains agile, innovative, and aligned with the organization's ever-evolving needs. High-performing teams constantly ask themselves, "*What's next?*"

Ask yourself and your team:

- What's next for us?

- How can we leverage our successes to reach new heights?

- What skills, habits, or strategies do we need to develop to continue growing?

By regularly asking these questions, you will inspire your team to stay curious, ambitious, and future-focused. This ensures that the team remains motivated and prepared to tackle the challenges that lie ahead.

Setting new goals

Goals are the compass that guides the team's direction. Whether it's improving communication, driving innovation, or enhancing team culture, setting new objectives helps keep the team engaged and motivated. To set new goals effectively, take these steps:

- Revisit the organization's overarching mission and ensure the team's goals align with it.

- Collaboratively define clear milestones and timelines to hold each other accountable.

- Schedule regular check-ins to track progress and make adjustments along the way.

Sustaining momentum

Momentum is the fuel that drives teams forward. To keep it alive, reinforce the organization's vision, continue investing in team development, and create an environment where trust, feedback, and collaboration remain central to the team's identity.

The long game of leadership

Leadership is a long-term commitment, and perseverance is at the core of this journey. Even as team dynamics shift, new challenges emerge, and fresh leaders join the fold, the foundation you have built will help your team endure and thrive. The journey doesn't have a clear endpoint, but with resilience, trust, and shared purpose, your team will continue to grow and succeed.

Building a legacy

Leadership is not just about achieving short-term results—it's about building a legacy that will endure long after you've left. The work you do to create a winning leadership team will leave a lasting impact, shaping the culture and influencing future generations of leaders.

The ripple effect of leadership

When you invest in a strong, cohesive leadership team, you're not just shaping the individuals within the room—you're creating a ripple effect that spreads throughout the organization and beyond. A high-performing leadership team sets a standard of excellence that will:

- Inspire future leaders to embrace accountability, trust, and collaboration.

- Encourage teams across the organization to adopt these same high standards.

- Foster a culture where everyone feels empowered, valued, and aligned with a shared vision.

The reward of perseverance

While the challenges of building a leadership team are significant, the rewards are immeasurable. Watching your team grow, align, and succeed together is one of the most fulfilling aspects of leadership. It serves as a reminder that perseverance, patience, and resilience are always worth it.

Leaving something that lasts

Your leadership is not defined solely by the results you achieved in the moment. It is defined by the foundation you've laid, the culture you've cultivated, and the future leaders you've inspired along the way. Your legacy is built on the strength of the team you've developed.

Conclusion

Building a winning leadership team is one of the most demanding, yet rewarding, undertakings a leader can embark upon. It requires perseverance through setbacks, gratitude for the progress made, and an unwavering commitment to the shared vision.

The journey is never linear, and it's never truly finished. As new challenges arise and new leaders come on board, the work continues. But for those who remain committed to the process, the reward is a leadership team that endures, thrives, and drives the organization toward lasting success.

Leadership is hard. The hours are long, the demands are unrelenting, and the weight of responsibility can feel overwhelming. But the effort is worth it. Building a team that trusts one another, shares a common vision, and works tirelessly toward a shared goal is a gift—one that extends far beyond individual achievements.

So, stay encouraged. Keep going! Much like the labor of childbirth, the process of building and sustaining a winning leadership team will test you, challenge you, and at times, bring you to tears. Embrace these challenges as opportunities to learn, grow, and become better. Celebrate progress, no matter how small. Invest in your people, trust the process, and remain steadfast in your pursuit of excellence. In the end, the legacy you leave will be defined not by your personal efforts alone but by the collective strength of your leadership team—now primed to win, and worth every moment of labor.